P9-DUP-893

"This pithy and profound author excels himself in this contemporary missions classic. Peter pulls no punches in describing the Jordan family journey out of their Montreal mansion comfort zone, into the front lines of a family in missions. His more sober moments of deep personal revelation, conviction, and repentance are skillfully intertwined with a sense of humor unique to this author. You will both laugh and cry as you journey with them deeper into the Great Commission. You will also be deeply challenged by the simple lifestyle of humility, faith, and obedience modeled by their family's journey into their destiny. Barbara and I have been privileged to be a part of this journey and blessed to know and work alongside such precious people as Peter and Donna."

DR. BRUCE THOMPSON
Founding dean of the College of Counseling and Health Care, University of the Nations

"I have known and been involved with the Jordan family for almost thirty years. They have inspired and challenged me along with countless others to carefully listen to God's voice and passionately pursue a commitment to become everything that we can be for the purpose of giving ourselves away. Theirs is an incredible story of what God can do with one ordinary family, totally committed to him. Their story will not only touch your life; it will revolutionize it."

DAN SNEED
International Bible teacher and author

"'The Jordans are leaving for the mission field!' Thirty-four years ago that news came as a major shock to us all. But to play a supporting role in their ministry all these years, and seeing God's hand at work in them and through them, has enabled our church to participate in this worldwide call to serve. An amazing account of the faithfulness of our heavenly Father."

MICHAEL BROWN
Elder, Bethel Chapel, Pointe Claire, Quebec

"It's been well over thirty years since I watched the Lord take a happy, prosperous, middle-class Canadian family out of their comfort zone and send them on a life-time adventure. This is the real thing—sacrifice, danger, challenge, excitement, and fulfillment! Careful! By reading their story you might also hear that still small voice calling you forth . . . just like Peter and Donna and their children back in 1976. Their story will show you that it's possible even with four children, and that you, too, can have the adventurous and challenging life as a missionary family."

PAUL HAWKINS
International teacher, Youth With A Mission

"*The Last Thing I'd Ever Do* aptly describes the unique profile of this wonderful couple who left their comfortable life in French Canada to live in a tent in the Pacific, listening for God's guidance in every move they have taken. I met Donna and Peter in 1985 and became their student in 1988 in Kona, Hawaii, Crossroads DTS. My life has been different ever since. I continue to value their mentorship, their friendship, and their prayers. This book will nourish not only your spirit but also your journey as you listen to God's word. Buy it, read it, and learn from the many lessons and miracles that appear on these pages."

RAYE KASS, PHD
Professor of applied human sciences; program director, Centre for Human Relations and Community Studies, Concordia University, Montreal, Quebec

The

LAST THING
I'D EVER DO

My Family's Adventure into
Faith and Missions

Peter Jordan

Foreword by
LOREN & DARLENE CUNNINGHAM

YWAM Publishing
Seattle, Washington

YWAM Publishing is the publishing ministry of Youth With A Mission. Youth With A Mission (YWAM) is an international missionary organization of Christians from many denominations dedicated to presenting Jesus Christ to this generation. To this end, YWAM has focused its efforts in three main areas: (1) training and equipping believers for their part in fulfilling the Great Commission (Matthew 28:19), (2) personal evangelism, and (3) mercy ministry (medical and relief work).

For a free catalog of books and materials, call (425) 771-1153 or (800) 922-2143. Visit us online at www.ywampublishing.com.

The Last Thing I'd Ever Do: My Family's Adventure into Faith and Missions
Copyright © 2011 by Peter Jordan

Published by YWAM Publishing
a ministry of Youth With A Mission
P.O. Box 55787, Seattle, WA 98155

First printing 2011

All rights reserved. No part of this book may be reproduced in any form without permission in writing from the publisher, except in the case of brief quotations in critical articles or reviews.

Library of Congress Cataloging-in-Publication Data has been applied for.

Unless otherwise noted, Scripture quotations are taken from the NEW AMERICAN STANDARD BIBLE®, Copyright © 1960, 1962, 1963, 1968, 1971, 1972, 1973, 1975, 1977, 1995 by The Lockman Foundation. Used by permission.

"Faith" by JoEllyn Wright used by permission. Last stanza by John H. Stammis and Daniel B. Towner.

ISBN 978-1-57658-557-3

Printed in the United States of America

To
Laurance Edward Jordan, 1889–1963,
&
Margaret Frohawk Phillips, 1899–1952,
who gave their lives to China and who gave me life.

I am blessed to be able to say that I was "Made in China."

Faith

Faith is the substance of what you can't see
Faith is the birthplace of your destiny
Watching and waiting for what is to be
Faith is the victory

So if you feel helpless and out of control
You're right where He wants you to be
Walking by faith, learning to wait
In total dependency

Faith is the fight that will finish the race
Faith must be birthed in the most barren place
Faith takes His promise while trusting His grace
Faith is a frightening place

So if you feel helpless and out of control
It means you're in good company
Children of Abraham, born of his seed
Part of the great family

Trust and obey, for there's no other way
To be happy in Jesus
But to trust and obey

—JoEllyn Wright, from her album *The Journey*

Contents

Foreword

Peter and Donna are like family to us. We have known them for more than thirty years, have worked closely with them, and are witnesses to much of what is recounted here.

The Last Thing I'd Ever Do is an inspiring read. Peter shares with candor and clarity both the inward and outward journey of his life, which will take you from China to Canada to the islands of the sea. But it is also a how-to book—a book about relationships and what happens to a family when the parents uproot the children from a comfortable lifestyle and take them to the rigors of a pioneering missionary life. It is a book that spells out what is required to walk in righteousness with great transparency and integrity. It is a laugh-and-cry book, as you relive the ups and downs of one family's journey from early pioneering to maturity.

Donna and Peter both have ministries that reach around the globe. They are a vital part of Youth With A Mission, and as individuals and as a family they represent much of what YWAM is all about, with our value of involving whole families called to missions.

It is for this reason that, with great joy, we commend to you Peter and Donna Jordan and *The Last Thing I'd Ever Do* at this time of celebrating YWAM's 50th birthday. This book will give you great insights for successful life and ministry into the next fifty years.

Loren and Darlene Cunningham
Founders, Youth With A Mission

Acknowledgments

To Donna, my faithful and loving wife these many years.

To our children, Laurie, Julie, Michelle, and Pete, without whom there would be little or no story to tell.

To our many friends over the years, who have, perhaps unwittingly, also given themselves to this tale of one family's adventure into a life of faith.

To Kevin Miller, who got me going on this long labor of love; and to Ryan Davis, who wrapped it up and tied the bow.

Oh yes! How can I forget Tom Bragg, who encouraged and believed?

Thank you all.

Peter Jordan
"The Hat" in Alberta, Canada
November 2010

Content in a Tent

Our family loved camping, but this was ridiculous—even if it was Hawaii. Mere days after leaving our comfortable home in Montreal with visions of palm trees and white sand beaches, we discovered that for the next three months, "home" was to be an old, leaky, olive-green army tent. It was pitched over a patch of lava rock—made slightly less jagged and lumpy by a musty carpet we had scrounged up. The only furniture that graced the sorry-looking shelter was iron bunk beds, until we added some storage "cabinets" fashioned from fruit crates from a local grocery store, plus a couple of unwanted school chairs from a bygone era. So this was what missionary training was all about.

Some sixty Youth With A Mission (YWAM) trainees—both families and singles—shared a lone cold-water shower, which was nothing more than a hose slung over a tarpaper frame. We also shared two toilets that defy description. Rather than assign one to each gender, they were divided according to bodily functions. To the left was the "Liquids Only" toilet, whose contents were channeled straight down into a lava tube, to be reduced to steam in the molten bowels of the volcano upon which we now lived. To the right was the "Solids Only" receptacle, whose contents were incinerated daily in a diesel-fueled fire.[1]

But we were in paradise, right? We could put up with minor inconveniences, such as the rain that fell frequently on what we laughingly called a farm, and the temperature that dipped into the fifties most nights because we were two thousand feet above sea level on the side of an inactive volcano. And living in a tent had its advantages. It had taken Donna, my wife, a full day each week to clean our four-bedroom, three-bathroom home in Montreal. Now it took her five minutes to sweep the lumpy rug, which served as a playground for mice, cockroaches, and poisonous centipedes.

Challenging though it sounds, I loved every minute of it. For the first time in my life I knew for certain that our family— me and Donna and our children, Laurie (fourteen), Julie (twelve), Michelle (eight), and Peter Jr. (six)—were right in the center of God's will. What a contrast to how I had lived my first forty-two years on earth!

In some ways, however, life in Hawaii felt strangely familiar. I had received ample preparation for rustic living as a boy, while a "guest" of the Japanese military in Shanghai during World War II. For almost three years our family of five—in China because my father worked as a missionary—was forced to live in a small room on the third floor of "D Block" in a Japanese internment camp. Before the war the building had been part of a Chinese school. During the war it served as a prison for 1,800 foreigners like us, who were caught in the wrong place at the wrong time when the Japanese took over most of Asia.

One of the best features of our little room was the window overlooking stretches of tidy green rice paddies with a Japanese-controlled airfield just beyond. Each day, scores of Mitsubishi

---

1. Dale Kauffman, who had just founded YWAM's children's ministry called King's Kids, incinerated the solids as his work duty.

Zero fighters took off, landed, and buzzed around us. I was spell-bound by this aerial activity and wasn't the least bit troubled by the meager dimensions of our prison home. During those days on the Hawaiian bush farm, I often reflected on my time as a POW. Living in a one-room tent was a breeze.

Our sojourn to Hawaii was the latest chapter in a long and adventurous story. I have never been accused of being a theologian, a philosopher, or an intellectual giant. As Professor Henry Higgins sang it so well in *My Fair Lady,* "I'm just an ordinary man." But I have been blessed with an extraordinarily diverse life. Change, you could say, has been my middle name. Born in China, imprisoned by the Japanese, and sent away to boarding school in England (my parents' home) for most of the next six years, I finally immigrated to Canada on my own at age seventeen. I had nothing but a few dollars in my pocket and contact information for one of my father's friends in Toronto.

Nevertheless, it didn't take long before I was gainfully employed. I enjoyed a long succession of jobs, my first being a stint as a stripper during the night shift in a paper box factory.[2] From there I moved on to summer camp, where I was labeled the worst counselor they ever had—I capsized a sailboat and discovered girls. Next I tried my hand in an advertising agency in Toronto, during which time I met Donna. Her father pointedly suggested that I further my education by going to university. Seeing as I wanted to marry his daughter, I thought it wise to comply. I returned to high school at age twenty to complete my credits, then suffered through two years of college with barely enough money for tuition and books. During my first year I eked out an existence as a live-in babysitter to a ten-year-old girl. During my second year I was a chauffeur and bodyguard for a wealthy elderly woman, who unfortunately passed away that year. I earned free meals by playing football, and I earned a bit of money as a

2. Using a pneumatic chisel, I stripped the borders off three-foot-high stacks of freshly printed, die-cut Chiclet chewing gum boxes. I also swept the floors. This "ministry" lasted just one winter.

pilot trainee with the Royal Canadian Air Force. This last step was my academic undoing. Flying airplanes extinguished the flickering flame of my meager academic aspirations.

Putting college behind me—though I was still in love with Donna—I went on to become a pilot in the Air Force. I was trained to shoot down Russian bombers during the Cold War, though I never saw any action. Then I became an air traffic controller, and a pilot once again, this time in the Royal Canadian Navy. On December 2, 1960, Donna and I were married in Guelph, near Toronto. When my flying career ended, I went into sales, starting with a business forms company and then selling advertising space in a national magazine. Finally, in my unremarkable though increasingly lucrative career, I became sales manager for a commercial printing company in Montreal. It felt like I had finally arrived. Donna and I assumed we would live happily ever after in suburbia. I had a good job, a beautiful home, two newer cars, a growing family, and a respectable position in our church. End of story, or so we thought.

Despite my missionary upbringing (or perhaps because of it), throughout my life I had either resisted God's intervention in my affairs or simply ignored him altogether. I had paid a price for my disobedience in missing God's best intentions for me and for my family.[3] But that was about to change. Change had defined the first half of my life, and it would also define the second. Rather than undergoing a series of random episodes, however, we would begin to see God's hand guiding and shaping the disordered events of our lives into a story that only he could imagine.

This book is my attempt to recount this story—both the challenges we faced and the amazing experiences of God's grace and provision, which continue to this day. It is, more importantly, a testimony of God's faithfulness at all times.

---

3. As Bible teacher Joy Dawson put it so clearly in a lecture I heard, "For obedience to be true obedience, it cannot be delayed, incomplete, or grudgingly carried out."

This book is for any individual or family who is considering a similar journey in obedience to God's call. It is for those who are in the thick of it right now, who have taken the plunge but may have started to waver. It is for those who have "been there, done that," and who still bear the scars of battle—for it is a battle. Above all, this book is for anyone who needs encouragement to follow Jesus' call—to do whatever, wherever, whenever, and with whomever he says. It is said that many are called, but few are packing. I want to see more people packing—literally and figuratively, prepared in every way for God's call.

— Chapter 1 —

Fat, Dumb, and Happy

P eter!" I heard my name spoken clearly and distinctly by a
male voice. It was 1976, and I was sitting alone in my plush
ninth-floor office in downtown Montreal. I had my feet up on the
desk while I read *Time* magazine during lunch hour. I glanced
around. The door to my office was closed. So where did the voice
come from? I looked out the window behind me, thinking that
perhaps a window washer was playing a trick. No one was there.
I got out of my chair and opened my office door. No one was outside, either. Even the secretaries were at lunch. I sat down again,
puzzled. I was certain it hadn't been my imagination; someone
had definitely called my name.

A scripture reference flashed through my mind. Weird,
I thought. This had never happened to me. Out of curiosity I
pulled a tiny King James New Testament out of my jacket pocket
and opened it to 1 Corinthians 7, the chapter containing the
verse that had entered my mind. Even before I opened the black,
leather-bound testament, however, I knew what the chapter was

about: marriage, divorce, and how it is "better to marry than to burn." Obviously, that had nothing to do with me—I was already married. Was I losing my mind?

Without reading the verse, I closed the little book and stuffed it back into my pocket. Had this happened a year earlier, it would have been the end of the matter. But a lot had changed over the past twelve months, and though I was still hesitant, my curiosity was piqued. A few moments later I pulled out the testament again. I had to see what the verse said.

Before I tell you what it said, I should give you some background. Ten months earlier, I had come to a crisis point. Our life in Montreal was pretty secure. We enjoyed most of the modern amenities that upwardly mobile people seek to attain. My job was assured (as long as I kept producing), my kids were coming along in school and sports, Donna and I were both active in the church, and to all appearances our marriage was humming along just fine. As the old air force saying goes, we were "fat, dumb, and happy." If you had asked me if I was a confessing Christian, I would have said yes. But the truth was, I hardly confessed my faith at all. In fact, I needed to do another kind of confessing.

My undoing had begun in 1974. After long posing as respectable churchgoers, we were disrupted by the concept of actually living out what we claimed to believe. This invasion of our world came from a young couple named Uli and Carol Kortsch. They were the national directors of YWAM Canada and had just moved to Montreal with their baby, Rachel, to prepare for what became the biggest Olympics outreach ever at the 1976 Summer Olympic Games. With great confidence Uli and Carol announced that up to two thousand young people from all over the world would descend on Montreal during the games to evangelize in the streets. *You gotta be kidding!* I thought.

But they weren't kidding, and by some strange turn of events Donna and I wound up on their advisory board. Pardon me? Advisors? To a couple of kids who didn't know enough *not* to tackle a monster project like this? Grudgingly—I was always grudging when it came to anything "spiritual" in those days—I agreed to teach the team a few things about planning, preparation, and purchasing a property to house the thousands they expected from the four corners of the earth.

All the while I felt like these kids didn't know enough to quit while they were ahead. I would have done well, however, to heed the old song from *The King and I*, which says, "If you become a teacher, by your pupils you'll be taught." Despite Uli and Carol's apparent inexperience, Donna and I were the ones who were in for a steep learning curve. Trusting God for everything and hearing his voice were staples of Uli and Carol's diet.

Their physical diet, on the other hand, was not nearly as nutritious. The Kortsches lived at the narrow end of the Christian charity pipeline. They were surrounded by people like me who easily could have elevated them above mere subsistence, but whose stingy giving was miring the gospel and hindering the kingdom of God in general. I reluctantly thrust twenty bucks in the offering every Sunday and thought I was doing my part.

My miserly nature was fueled in part by a spiritual awakening that Donna had shortly before we met Uli and Carol. The way that Uli and Carol listened to God made Donna hungry for more. But this did not rub off on me. In fact, I was threatened by it and started to withdraw from Donna regarding spiritual things. At first, she tried playing the role of the Holy Spirit to convict me, but when that approach didn't work, she wisely backed off and put her energy into praying for me (though I didn't know it at the time). God was starting to lovingly corner me; he wanted me to get my life together. And yet I wasn't ready to heed the whispers of his call. "Thank you very much," was my response, "but my life is going just fine. Let's not mess with a good thing."

Despite my protests, I now had three spiritual influences bearing down on me—Donna, the Kortsches, and the Holy Spirit himself. Resist as I might, I didn't stand a chance. I began to receive revelations of scriptural truths that had previously flown over my head. I also came under the conviction of the Holy Spirit. Had I been wrong? Could God's children hear his voice today? Did God not just convict us of sin but also speak to us at any time, anywhere, about anything? Maybe Uli, Carol, and—horrors—Donna were onto something. Maybe "living by faith," as my father had done his entire life, was possible for all believers.

I suffered many sleepless nights battling the Holy Spirit's wooing, which to me usually felt like a heavy burden of guilt and sin. One of my heaviest burdens had to do with work. I had a great deal of freedom in the way I ran my division of the company. I traveled a lot and had an unlimited expense account. I took full advantage of the "unlimited" part by padding my expenses and skimming pocket money. After all, everybody else was doing it, so I thought I might as well get my piece of the pie. But the Holy Spirit seemed to be saying, "No, that's stealing."

The Lord also reminded me of the diamond-encrusted watch I had given Donna on our tenth wedding anniversary. She had lost it some years later, and I had put in an insurance claim, receiving full value for it. Soon afterward we found the watch, but I never returned the insurance money.

Worse still was my thought life. A veritable gutter ran through the center of my mind. My inner world was a selfish place, and nobody else was allowed to trespass there, not even Donna. Somehow I was preserved from immoral relationships with other women, but I knew I was still fully guilty, seeing as Jesus said, "Anyone who looks at a woman lustfully has already committed adultery with her in his heart" (Matt. 5:28 NIV).

I lived under the heavy hand of conviction for several months. Then in September 1975 I attended a retreat for our church's Boys' Club, of which I was the leader. After lunch one day, an elder gave a short talk on commitment. It wasn't a particularly inspiring message—the guy next to me fell asleep—but it was my *kairos* moment, the moment God grabbed me. I began to ponder what commitment was all about, and thought that maybe I should recommit my life to God. But how could I recommit when I hadn't made a commitment to begin with? My entire

Christian life had been a sham, a way of looking respectable in the eyes of others.

When the elder finished his message, I went straight over to him and said I wanted to commit the remainder of my life to Christ, whatever that might mean. I prayed with him to this effect—a dangerous prayer indeed. That was on a Saturday.

The following Monday morning, I made an appointment to see the president of my company. After a few anxious hours, the time for our meeting arrived. With a severe case of the shakes, I knocked on the president's door, not knowing whether I would have a job when I walked out of his office. With eyes hidden by thick horn-rimmed glasses, he sat magisterially behind a huge oak desk. At that moment the desk seemed as wide and long as a football field. The president listened in silence as I confessed to stealing from the company. I said I was sorry, and that I would be willing to figure out how much I had taken and pay it all back.

When I was finished, he came out from behind his desk with his hand extended and a smile on his round face. "Thank you very much," he said. Then, to my consternation, he brushed the whole matter aside and changed the subject to business. To this day I wonder about his strange response. Was the practice of padding expense accounts an unwritten perk? Or was my boss guilty of the same sin? I'll never know. It doesn't matter anyway, because I was finally free from the dreaded guilt weighing so heavily on my conscience. I knew I would never steal from the company again.

But there was more sin to dump. Next up was Donna's "lost and found" diamond watch. I wrote an apology to the insurance company. I included a check for the full amount they had paid me plus interest for the years I had delayed in returning it. I received an appreciative letter in return. Donna rejoiced with me as I off-loaded more sin.

The next item on my list was unfortunately not quite so simple: the lustful thoughts that constantly ran through my mind. Instead of confessing my sin to another person, as I had done with the expense account and the watch, I thought I could just confess to God and everything would be okay. Wrong. Confessing something like this to God doesn't make it go away. No sooner had I confessed than outside influences—movies, books, television, scantily clad women walking down the street—conspired to stir up unclean thoughts. I was distraught. Why wasn't I free from my sin? I had yet to learn God's ways of purifying the mind. I also had no clue that there was an enemy who would not let go of me in these matters. This was to be a lengthy, secret, no-holds-barred fight. I was a scrawny, ill-equipped rookie squaring off against a being who knew every trick in the book, every way to tantalize, torture, and take me down again and again. This being is, of course, the enemy of our souls, who never gives up as long as we allow weaknesses in our armor. I had much to learn.

Apart from this ongoing struggle, things started to go well for me spiritually. For the first time in a long while, Donna and I were on the same page. We were spiritually "packing" for whatever God might have for us. We began to pray together. Unlike before, I was now open to stepping out of our comfortable lifestyle to do something that God had initiated. As the city of Montreal readied herself for the Olympic Games set for July 1976, we readied ourselves as well. We didn't know what it would look like, but we both felt that God was preparing us for service. Since we had both worked in youth ministries at our church, we assumed it would have something to do with ministering to the next generation. Our growing association with Uli and Carol's Olympics outreach seemed like a natural fit. Where would things go from there? In our minds we were packed and ready to go. We just didn't know where.

Now you have a better idea of the circumstances when I found myself in my office hearing a voice and having a scripture reference flash through my brain. "And they that use this world, as not abusing it: for the fashion of this world passeth away" (1 Cor. 7:31 KJV). That was the verse. To put it in more modern English: "those who use the things of the world, as if not engrossed in them. For this world in its present form is passing away" (NIV). I wasn't quite sure what it meant, but I sensed that God was alerting me that our family was about to go through some radical changes. I was so shaken by this incident that I didn't tell anyone about it, not even Donna. I was afraid I would be seen as crazy or as a religious fanatic.

So I continued forward. In a few short days the Olympic Games would be upon us, and we would be leaving our comfortable home to bunk with the nearly two thousand mostly young people from around the world. Uli and Carol's vision had come true, and I was starting to believe that God speaks personally to his children, even today.

— Chapter 2 —

Let the Games Begin!

The 1976 Summer Olympic Games were the games of Nadia Comaneci, the lithe and limber fourteen-year-old gymnast from Romania. She captured the hearts of the world as she scored seven perfect tens and won three gold medals, including the prestigious All-Around. The games also marked a watershed in my life—the point at which I ceased struggling against God's will and finally let him take me and my family in the direction that *he* had for us.

As the world's eyes focused on Montreal, our family packed up and moved out to the YWAM base a few miles outside the city, where there was an influx of young people. One hundred came from Finland in a chartered aircraft. Seventy-six arrived from Egypt. Scores came from South Africa, and many hundreds from Canada, the United States, and other nations. They hitch-hiked, flew, and drove in cars, rickety old vans, and dilapidated school buses. The crew that had gathered to spread the Good News on the streets of Montreal was motley indeed.

Three days before the outreach officially began, more than four hundred had already arrived. This raised a pressing question: what was to be done with so many young people when the program had yet to begin? With so much time on their hands, they might get into trouble. (Idle hands are the devil's workshop!) The outreach leaders felt the Lord saying this was an ideal opportunity for teaching. The next day all four hundred of us sat down on the hardwood floor of a gymnasium. For two hours Paul Hawkins, a leader in YWAM, taught on intercessory prayer. Incredibly, the time flew by as though it were just a few minutes. I had never experienced anything like it! I was the kind of guy who had a hard time with any sermon over twenty-five minutes. Plus I had always considered intercession a necessary but boring part of the Christian life.

After his message, Paul broke us up into groups, each led by an experienced intercessor. Bruce Heckman, a rather serious-looking young American missionary to the Middle East,[1] was appointed to guide our group of six. We started by asking God to reveal anything in our hearts that might hinder us from hearing him speak. We wanted to pray about the things *he* wanted us to pray about, not just the usual "shopping list" of items we thought were important. God led us to pray for the Philippines and also to intercede on behalf of others and "stand in the gap."[2]

Following the most dynamic hour of prayer in my life, I lingered with Donna to talk to Bruce. We told him about our situation and asked him to pray with us, to see if the Lord would reveal something to him. Donna and I sensed that God might be leading us to serve with YWAM, but we weren't certain. The three of us asked the Lord if this was the right course. After we opened our eyes, neither Donna nor I had clear guidance, just the feeling that we were on the right track. As for Bruce, his response was cryptic: "God spoke to me, but I'm not released to

1. He eventually served there for eighteen years.
2. See Ezekiel 22:30.

tell you what he said just yet." Puzzled, Donna and I parted company with Bruce and went to lunch. PBJs (peanut butter and jelly sandwiches) were the regular fare for this outreach.

By the time the official program began, 1,800 adventurous missionaries had gathered from around the globe, far exceeding our capacity to house them. Most of the single women slept on the floor of a hockey rink (the ice had been removed for the summer). Dear old Wally Wenge, a YWAM leader and ever the organizer, taped off hundreds of seven-by-four-foot rectangles on the concrete floor, one for each woman. The guys slept wherever a corner or a tent could be found. Families slept in school dorms. We stayed with Uli and Carol in a tiny caretaker's cottage adjacent to a former girls' school, and our kids slept outside in our tent trailer. It was a scorching summer, and Carol, who was hugely pregnant with their second child, struggled to get around, let alone be a den mother to hundreds of guests.

For a full week prior to the actual start of Games, we continued our training. Each morning, afternoon, and evening we filed into a nearby high school, munched on PBJs, and listened to teachings. We heard up-to-the-minute reports and thrilling stories about real missionaries, some of whom were among us. These were ordinary people doing extraordinary things under God's guidance. My comfortable cage was rattled with God's truth as I listened to Loren Cunningham, Joy Dawson, Don Stephens, Brother Andrew, Floyd McClung, and others. One session, during which we fasted involuntarily from the dreaded PBJs, lasted seven hours. God moved among us powerfully in a way that I had never before witnessed.

Late one night, Donna and I drove back from the meetings, pondering a challenge from Loren Cunningham. He said that as followers of Jesus we were called to give up our rights. We had never heard anything like this. Society seemed to be clamoring for *more* rights, starting with noble liberties such as women's rights and civil rights for all shapes and shades of people. But others had taken things further—demanding, for example, the right to live immoral lives, and to be respected for it, no less. For the most part, the church just stood by and watched, occasionally heckling from the sidelines. Loren's teaching was revolutionary because it went in exactly the opposite direction. Jesus led the way by relinquishing all that he had—why couldn't we give up a few things too?

As I parked the car, Donna and I asked the Lord what he wanted us to give up. We desired to "clear the decks" to be free to go into missions training for a year or so. A few things came to mind: our house, our cars, my job, family, friends, even reputation. We hesitantly named each of these and responded, "Yes, Lord." Surprisingly, instead of feeling loss, we both felt a lightening in our spirits, that weights and encumbrances had been released. Then I prayed a risky prayer, one that I would never have dreamed of uttering a few months before: "Lord, if we are to join YWAM, give us three signs. And let one of them be that our children will want to go." Though I felt led to speak this prayer, I wondered if I had crossed a line with God.

In all of this, Donna and I were in perfect unity, excited about the faith adventure into which we were stepping. We learned that in a few weeks YWAM would be running a six-month school at the headquarters for Asia and the Pacific in Kona, Hawaii. If we wanted to join the mission, we had to attend. Hawaii? Missionary training? What would our friends and family think? Would they laugh at us, thinking we had taken leave of our senses? It didn't matter, because we were flushed with new vision. We felt like Gideon must have felt when he put out the fleece, asking for confirmation that the Lord was calling him.[3]

We had to wait two weeks, almost until the end of the outreach, for all three signs to come. The first sign came through another question: "Lord, if we go, what should we do with our house—sell it or rent it?" His answer came one day while I was in my office in Montreal taking a break from the outreach to

3. See Judges 6:37–40.

catch up on some paperwork. I sensed God telling me to look in the "Houses Wanted to Let" section of the classified ads in *The Montreal Gazette.* I was horrified! *The Gazette* was the rival newspaper to our sister company's *Montreal Star.* I would never read *The Gazette,* much less be seen with it. I didn't even know if it had such a section in the classifieds. But I was learning to heed the voice of God. So no matter how outrageous this directive sounded, I decided to obey.

As unobtrusively as possible, I rummaged around the outer office searching for the hated newspaper. Perhaps someone had smuggled one to work and discarded it in a wastebasket. Sure enough, I found one. Hiding it under my jacket, I took it back to the privacy of my office. With the door closed, I searched for the "Houses Wanted to Let" section. There it was. And it contained only one listing: an executive moving to Montreal wanted to rent a home. But not just any home. If I had written an ad describing our house, I couldn't have done a better job! The location, the size of the house, the number of bedrooms—every feature the executive mentioned matched our home. And he wanted to rent it for about a year!

You can imagine the speed at which I drove back to tell Donna the good news. I also summoned up the courage to tell her about my lunchtime encounter with the Lord a few weeks earlier. She was amazed and excited that I was finally hearing from God, though a little hurt that I had not shared this with her right after it happened.[4]

Meanwhile, the Olympics moved along with no major security crisis, as had been the case four years earlier in Munich, Germany, where eleven Israeli athletes had been murdered by Palestinian Black September terrorists. Incidentally, the Munich Games were the occasion for YWAM's first Olympics outreach: one thousand young people gathered from all over the world to share the love of

---

4. I have since discovered that in the Bible the Lord usually spoke audibly to people when he needed to wake them up and get their attention. He sure got mine!

Jesus. Following the murders, they were instrumental in calming fears by holding a "Jesus Love March" through the streets of the city. Now the Montreal outreach—a coordinated effort of fifty-one ministry organizations, including YWAM—reported many coming to salvation and other miracles on the streets of the city.

As the outreach wound down, we had received an answer to our first question: we were to rent, not sell, our house. Then came the second sign. Our kids ran up to us excitedly and asked, "Are we going to Hawaii?" During a bus ride to one of the children's events, they had heard some leaders' wives talking about the possibility of our joining the mission in Hawaii. We replied carefully, "We're praying about it right now." We didn't need to ask what our kids thought. Julie, twelve years old and a budding three-sport athlete; competitive Michelle, age eight; and active Peter, almost six, would go anywhere with us. Laurie, our oldest at age fourteen, was the one we were concerned about. Though she joined in the excitement of the others, we knew that leaving her friends would be difficult. She had struggled at school and was having difficulty with her eyesight, both of which undermined her self-confidence. But she seemed willing, so we took that as a positive answer.

As the final day of the outreach arrived, we still hadn't received our third sign from the Lord. All systems indicated "Go," yet we lacked that final confirmation. Had we missed it? Had I been presumptuous in expecting God to give us three signs? Was I experiencing a midlife crisis? Or were we heading into a cult? After all, at that point YWAM was virtually unknown to the body of Christ, and some who were aware of the organization were leery of it. For that reason we had not dared to mention our plans to anyone outside the outreach bubble in which we had been living for the past three weeks.

With all of these questions and concerns buzzing around our minds, we headed over to the cafeteria for the final lunch of the outreach. As several hundred of us funneled through the entrance, I caught sight of a man battling against the tide of hungry lunch-goers. It was Bruce Heckman, the young man who had prayed with us at the beginning of the outreach, and whom we hadn't seen since. Bruce made straight for us and, with no preliminary small talk, asked, "Has God shown you what to do yet?"

Amid the jostling, milling, and famished throng, I replied, "We think so. We believe we are to go to Hawaii."

With eyes reflecting the weightiness of what he was about to say, Bruce responded, "Yes, that's what the Lord told me three weeks ago." Greatly relieved that God had delivered our third and final sign, we thanked Bruce. Then he moved past us, struggling against the surge of people. We never saw him again.[5]

Now it was confirmed: we were to become missionary pioneers. When we told our family and friends, some of them did think we were nuts. They assumed that once I got this out of my system I would settle down and resume a normal productive life. But they didn't realize that my genes destined me not to settle for the ordinary. And Donna's weren't much different.

---

5. Bruce now lives in Pennsylvania with his wife, Joyce, and their children.

— Chapter 3 —

Our Pioneer Roots

My father, Laurance Edward Jordan, was born in the blue-collar town of Sittingbourne, England, in the eastern part of the county of Kent, near Canterbury and its famous cathedral. He was always proud to be known as a "Man of Kent," as distinct from a "Kentish Man."[1]

Dad came from humble beginnings, one of seven brothers who labored in a paper mill. They had one sister, Kate, who was an angel to her brothers. Just before the start of World War I, when Dad was still a young man, he became a Christian. The details of this decision are lost in the mists of time, but soon he was active in ministry among his newly adopted spiritual kinsmen, the Plymouth Brethren. The Brethren had assembled in the

---

1. Kentish Men were those born west of the River Medway, closer to London. Dad gave me the clear understanding—with a twinkle in his eye—that they were an inferior class of people. It seems that some 1,500 years earlier, the Men of Kent had more stoutly resisted William the Conqueror than the Kentish Men who weakly surrendered. Old prejudices die hard.

1820s in the city of Plymouth in southwestern England. Early leaders included such notables as George Müller, J. N. Darby, and Anthony Norris Groves, men who broke away from the traditional churches of the day because they were forbidden to share the Lord's Supper and other ceremonies across denominational lines. Sadly, after a few generations this beautiful Brethren flower started to wilt, dropping its seeds onto the fertile soil of division. Over time, some fifty expressions of the Brethren sprang up because of nit-picky interpretations of minor doctrinal details. Most of these groups would have little or nothing to do with each other, much less the wider church. Yet today, there is still a faithful remnant of those early Brethren.

Discipled and schooled in God's Word, Dad was soon preaching and teaching in the surrounding areas of Kent, often with just his Bible, a tent, and a bicycle. His life of total dependence on God had begun. In his early twenties, and with no formal training, he felt God's call to the mission field. Forsaking the comforts and security of England, he boarded a ship bound for China, that far-off land of mystery and history.

The voyage to Shanghai took three months. Today, with modern jet airliners that can take you almost anywhere in the world within twenty-four hours, such a voyage is difficult to imagine. After stops in some of Britain's far-flung outposts like Aden (now in Yemen), Bombay (now called Mumbai), Ceylon (now called Sri Lanka), Singapore, and Hong Kong, Dad would have been ready for some solid earth beneath his feet. From Shanghai he began the journey inland, where, for the next five years, he immersed himself in the Chinese language and culture. During that time he was isolated from his native English culture. Airmail didn't exist in those days. Letters took as long to travel around the world as passengers on ships did.

Following his five-year term, Dad returned to England for twelve well-earned months of furlough. Though it was supposed to be restful, he was rarely at rest. He spent the year visiting supporters, raising the required prayer and provision for his next five years away from Shakespeare's "Scepter'd Isle," and recruiting others to come with him.

Now in his early thirties, he also met and fell in love with Margaret Frohawk Phillips from the town of Fakenham in the county of Norfolk, 120 miles north of London. Tall, attractive, and statuesque, Margaret was an athletic young woman with a slightly "roamin'" nose, courtesy of an errant field hockey ball taken flush between her eyes. She was ten years Laurance's junior and was the product of a long line of Christians from the same Brethren lineage under whose mission board my father was serving. She was a woman of grace and truth. No guile lay hidden within her heart. But there was a problem: Margaret's father didn't want his young daughter running off to China with some reckless man from the lower working class of English society, even if he was sincere about his calling. Discouraged, Laurance figured he stood no chance of winning this fair maiden's hand, so he backed off.

Laurance must have had a heavy heart as he trudged aboard ship for the three-month voyage back to China. He had little hope that Margaret would wait five years for him, given the abundance of eligible young suitors knocking at her door. Nevertheless, in obedience to God—and his mission board—he set sail on a dreary winter day that well matched his feelings of desolation. One can only imagine how he felt as the enormous mooring ropes dropped into the water, severing all connection between him and the woman he loved.

Southward sailed the despondent missionary, past France, Portugal, Spain, through the Strait of Gibraltar, and into the Mediterranean Sea. From there the ship carved its wake eastward until Egypt lay to starboard. The liner safely negotiated the huge locks of the Suez Canal, then traveled down the length of the Red Sea to Aden, its first port of call. So far the voyage had taken almost three weeks.

Somewhere in the reaches of the seas just spanned, during the lonely night watches, something fell into place for the man

who was to become my father. Whether he regretted not proposing to Margaret, or whether God spoke to him through a dream,
we'll never know. What we do know is that the downhearted
missionary was galvanized into action. He jumped ship in Aden
and caught the next ocean liner back to England, arriving several
weeks later. Without delay he made his way to Margaret's home
and proposed. To his uncontained delight, she accepted. What
Margaret's family thought of this alliance is not recorded.

Plans jelled quickly. Before long, Dad reembarked for China,
this time with a much lighter heart, because a year later Margaret
was to follow him halfway around the world to the mysterious
Orient. Sure enough, twelve months later, amid Chinese pomp
and splendor, the two became one. This union produced four
children over a span of ten years: John, Ruth, and Theodore all
came within the first six years of the marriage; I arrived six years
after Theodore.

Despite this radical courtship, I don't remember my dad as a
romantic. He adhered to the missionary priorities of that day—
God-ministry-family, in that order. Romantic or not, Dad pressed
on despite huge challenges and adversity, living obediently and
trusting his Lord. God's provision through his mission board was
sometimes adequate and sometimes delayed. I remember walking to school with no shoes for a few days when I was about eight
years old, but that only happened on one occasion. I never heard
my parents complain about lack of finances, though times were
often tough. My dad saw fruit from his ministry, but most of his
time was spent planting seed and watering it.

Perhaps a consistent life lived in obedience and trust is in
itself a form of spiritual warfare, for Paul speaks of "stand[ing]
firm against the schemes of the devil" (Eph. 6:11). No matter
what happened, Dad never allowed the forces of darkness to
deflect him from God's will.

The McAllister clan—Donna's ancestors—had the pioneering
spirit as well. In 1833 they made the difficult emigration

from Scotland to Canada. After crossing the Atlantic Ocean, which took eleven weeks, their unscrupulous captain dumped them on the banks of the mighty St. Lawrence River and made off with all their belongings. The family made their way upriver, eventually settling on farmland near Montreal. Robert, Donna's great-great-grandfather, was ten years old upon their arrival.

Around 1850 Robert, now married with five children, moved farther west and rented one hundred acres of virgin land west of Toronto. There, he and his wife, Jane, had six more children, including George, Donna's great-grandfather. The family lived in a one-story log house. In 1863, when George was six, Robert, Jane, and their eleven children moved farther north and purchased two hundred acres. In those days, trees were the enemy of the settlers and had to be cut down before the land could be farmed. This provided Robert McAllister with an abundance of logs. Wanting plenty of employment for his sons, he set up a sawmill and blacksmith shop. Soon both businesses were thriving as he supplied lumber and horseshoes for the burgeoning population.

Milling and blacksmithing weren't the only things at which Robert excelled. He also fathered one more child—twelve in total—all of whom survived into adulthood. Donna's great-grandfather, George, was number eight.

When the McAllisters arrived in Canada, they were good Scottish Presbyterians. But in the 1870s a couple of itinerant Plymouth Brethren evangelists came along and converted the entire family, together with some neighbors. They established a Brethren assembly. Robert and Jane McAllister regularly said a prayer from Psalm 78:5–7: "That they should teach [the law] to their children, that the generation to come might know, even the children yet to be born, that they may arise and tell them to their children, that they should put their confidence in God, and not forget the works of God, but keep His commandments." This prayer has borne much fruit, even to this day. Four of Robert and Jane's children married Elliots, and out of one of those unions came Jim Elliot, one of the five missionary martyrs in Ecuador in 1956.

As further testimony to God's faithfulness, in 1996 almost four hundred McAllisters held a reunion in Guelph, Ontario, at the birthplace of Donna's grandfather John. I went along with Donna and our three daughters and was moved by this huge gathering to honor their predecessors. Representatives from all but one of the twelve "tribes" were present, drawn from all over North America and Japan. Only one family seemed to have drifted away from the faith of their fathers. It was a privilege to witness what God had done through the faithful prayers of a righteous husband and wife on behalf of the *generations yet to be born*.

Donna's mother, Gwendoline (Gwen) Mabel McAllister, married Donald Henry Wilson, an out-of-work artist from Windsor, Ontario. Donald's father was an engineer on the railroad, but Donald had a creative bent and had gotten a job in an advertising agency across the border in Detroit. He sketched and painted cars for the burgeoning automobile industry. Then came the disastrous stock market crash of 1929 and the start of the Great Depression. Donald couldn't find any creative work. Out of desperation he took employment in the lumber business (since he had married the boss's daughter). While the job put plenty of bread on the table, Donald, the gifted artist, was neither happy nor fulfilled. Eventually, he bought the business from his father-in-law, but later sold it and returned to his first love—art. He bought an expensive Linhoff camera and began doing portrait photography, for which he won much acclaim.

I landed upon this family on a raw and snowy day, still in my teens and fresh off the boat (FOB) from the "Old Country" of England.[2] The moment I set eyes on Donna—a vivacious redhead with sparkling and mischievous blue eyes—I knew she was the one for me. But two details prevented me from marrying her straightaway: she was only two days past her fifteenth birthday (I was nineteen), and her dad believed I needed more schooling and

2. FOB is a term still used to describe new immigrants. Less welcoming derivatives were DP for "displaced person" and JC for "I Justa Come"—unkindly aimed at Italians and mocking their accent.

a good job before I thought about marriage. For the next seven years I felt like Jacob laboring under the hard hand of Laban for the right to marry his daughter Rachel.[3] I'm happy to report that unlike Laban, my father-in-law didn't slip me a substitute wife when the long-awaited day arrived! Instead he blessed me. And besides, his only remaining single daughter, Martha, was already promised to her longtime friend Dave McPhee.

So it was, on December 2, 1960, the Phillips/Jordan family united with the McAllister/Wilson clan through our marriage. Unknown to Donna and me, we were destined to follow in our forebears' pioneering footsteps. After fifteen years of marriage and with four children, we were about to become missionaries like my parents. But instead of a mysterious land like China, we were off to tropical islands with swaying palms and pristine beaches lapped by sparkling azure waves. Most people associated Hawaii with rest and relaxation. So how were we to explain that God had called us there, not to vacation, but to do missionary work? With our call confirmed, we were about to find out.

3. See Genesis 29.

Chapter 4

Packing

With God's direction clear and our decision made, we faced the daunting task of tidying up our affairs. But instead of feeling stressed about moving, we were excited. For the first time in our lives we were obeying God in every detail. Although this was new territory for us, we were full of faith. We needed to be! God had given us the essentials, but he hadn't shared many of the specifics. We had a destination and a short-term time frame; what lay beyond that, we didn't have a clue. Even so, we had more to go on than Abraham did![1]

In addition to packing up the house, we still needed to rent it out. The executive whose advertisement I had read changed his plans because his company no longer wanted him to move to Montreal. But we still believed that God had directed us to rent our house, not sell it. We had to decide what to do with furniture and other items and pack up the necessities for our missionary training. We had to inform our church of our decision. And I

1. See Genesis 12:1.

needed to resign from my job. We had to do all of this plus many other things in just five weeks: our training started in early September, and it was already August.

When the Olympics outreach ended, I made an appointment with the president of my company. The next day I was ushered into his spacious and beautifully appointed office—where only a few months earlier I had confessed my sin of stealing—and handed him my resignation letter. As soon as he read it, he looked up at me over his glasses and said, "I've been expecting this." Evidently he had noticed a change in me over the past year.[2]

Donna's family did not like this wild idea of us packing up in the prime of life—with *their* grandchildren, no less—and heading off to parts unknown. They believed that family was meant to stay together. Hadn't we already left them once before to move three hundred miles away to Montreal? Donna's dad thought we were joining a cult. Her mom remained mostly silent, which we took to be approval. And Donna's younger sister Martha was distraught, thinking she would never see Donna, her hero, again.

I had recently become an elder at Bethel, our church, and we knew the people loved us. But we put that love to the test when we announced that we believed God was calling us into overseas missions and that we were planning to leave soon. The elders said, "We've been praying that we could send out missionaries

2. Several years later, when we were home on a short furlough, he invited me to an extravagant two-hour lunch at a fancy French restaurant in the heart of Old Montreal. After lunch, as he lit up a cigarette and took a sip of his coffee, it became clear why we were enjoying this amazing blend of good food and French ambience. "The company's not doing well; we've lost a lot of business," he said. "I'd like you to consider coming back." His offer wasn't too surprising. In the eight years of my employment I had taken the commercial printing division of the company from under half a million dollars annually to well over seven million annually. He thought I could bring it all back. I declined his offer as politely as I could, though I could have laughed in his face. To think that I would turn away from God's calling seemed like madness, even when at that point our mission base in Hawaii was experiencing major financial struggles.

from here, but we meant *young* missionaries! However, we can see that God has called you." Even though many had misgivings, everyone was gracious and loving. They sent us off with a farewell prayer, a blessing, and a set of quality luggage—but no indication that they would support us.

Despite our efforts, on the day of our departure our beautiful home of eight years lay empty with no prospective renters in sight. We felt that the Lord wanted the house to be rented by Christians so that a witness could be maintained in the neighborhood. That had kept us from advertising it for rent. The elders of our church said they would watch over it for us and try to find a renter while we were away. I was grateful for their commitment, but I must confess to a few germs of doubt in my heart. We knew we would be trusting God to provide for our family. But as we prepared to leave, no one had stepped forward to support us financially. Our assets at the time included a small company pension (which our elders had strongly advised us to put into a tax-free investment plan), a house that the Lord told us not to sell, and just enough money for thirty days of missionary training school. We sensed God whispering a simple but profound message: *Have faith.*

Then a strange thing happened. Just three weeks before setting off on this new journey, out of the blue, I was offered a job in Toronto. It was a position I had coveted for many years, it paid 30 percent more than I had been making in Montreal, and it would mean moving back to once-familiar territory. But why now, Lord?

I declined the offer. I've often wondered if it was the Lord's way of testing my resolve, or if it was the devil's attempt to deflect us from God's will. Over the years I have come to see that whenever a follower of Jesus makes a significant decision to obey his Master, something will come up as an alternative—usually a very tempting alternative.

In the midst of it all, Laurie, Julie, Michelle, and Peter approached our coming transplantation to Hawaii from different angles. But there was a genuine sense of excitement as we talked about all that the future might offer.

> Michelle remembers: *Being only eight years old, I was just excited. Having no idea what was ahead, I just trusted my mom and dad. I was excited about going somewhere new and excited about the plane trip, seeing as I'd never been on a plane before. I don't remember much more than that about my feelings before we left Montreal. I knew I would miss my best friend, Claudia, and all my relatives (although we saw each other only a couple of times a year anyway).*

> Julie remembers: *I don't even remember saying goodbye to my friends in Montreal. I guess my mind was more focused on the adventure ahead. Getting to Kona took a long time. The only thing I remember about the plane ride was that I won a birthday cake—and it wasn't even my birthday! I also remember feeling very "spiritual," because I found out there was a man on the plane who really was celebrating his birthday that day. His name was Nate Krupp, and he was also on his way to YWAM Kona with his family. So I, the good little missionary girl, laid down my rights and gave the birthday cake to him. From then on I knew the missionary life was for me and that I could handle anything!*

As our departure date approached, we began to take a series of blows. They continued even after we arrived in Hawaii, leading us to feel like some unseen force was contesting our decision. Discouragement was our enemy's preferred method of harassment. Four specific occasions stand out.

The first two blows came right before we climbed aboard the jumbo jet that would fly us into our future. On the drive to the airport we asked Donna's dad to pray for us. He did, but then he uttered a startling statement. "You know," he said, "my prayers go with you, but not my blessing." Thankfully, the kids were in another car and didn't hear their grandfather's proclamation. But it hit Donna and me like a curse. As you might expect, Donna dissolved into tears.

After a tearful family farewell, we dragged our assortment of four tightly crammed and roped teaboxes (made of thin plywood and previously used for shipping bulk tea) plus our brand-new luggage set given to us by our church, totaling twelve odd pieces of luggage, not including carry-ons! Sweating profusely, I presented our travel documents to a US Immigration and Customs officer. To his credit, he didn't just roar with laughter at our motley crew of a family—Donna, with tear-streaked face; me, panting heavily from hauling endless pieces of luggage; and the kids, excitedly anticipating they knew not what. Nor did the officer simply turn us around and send us home.

"What are you going to be doing?" he queried after consulting our documents.

"We'll be attending a training program," I replied as confidently as I could. I'd never had trouble entering the US before.

The expression on his face said, "You gotta be kidding!" But he didn't voice those words. Instead he asked, "And how are you going to support yourselves? How much money do you have? You can't work in the United States." I could see him eyeing our four school-age kids and thinking to himself, *How in the world will they be supported?*

I struggled to keep my facial muscles from jumping all over the place. Deep inside—or not so deep inside—I was panicking. I could imagine the consequences of being turned back and having to admit to our family and friends that we had "missed it"— that God hadn't really spoken to us. We had burned the bridges behind us, so what would we do if the officer wouldn't let us in? Tightness gripped my throat as I replied, "We have enough money for one month."

His rejoinder came quickly. "What will you do after that? You can't work!" This last declaration came with an air of finality. It was then that I realized US immigration policy does not include "living by faith" as a satisfactory reason for admittance to America. Then the look on the officer's face softened. "I'll allow you in for thirty days." With that, he stamped our passports and waved us on.

A small victory. Now we had permission to stay in the United States for one month, with just enough money to cover our expenses for that period of time. We were trusting God, I told myself. Nevertheless, we boarded the plane with a boiling mixture of emotions. Faith can be a frightening place.

— Chapter 5 —

Landing on the Moon

Our day traveling to Kona, Hawaii, was one of the longest and most difficult of our lives. *Long* because we passed through six time zones that stretched the daylight hours as we chased the sun westward. *Difficult* because we spent those hours crammed among hundreds of loud and festive vacationers while absorbing the horror of the apparent curse that Donna's dad had put on us by withholding his blessing. Donna's tears flowed freely throughout the ten-hour flight from Chicago to Honolulu.

Donna remembers: *When my dad said he would pray for me but not bless me, I was devastated. My friends and family were very important to me, so I wanted to please them, especially my dad. I was the third daughter, but I was "supposed" to be a son. My dad's name was Don, so they named me Donna. When we left for Kona, I knew a lot about God, but now I had to rely on him completely. There was so much I didn't understand, but I had to trust God. I can see why my dad was concerned, but God's grace was on us. My mother was a little more understanding. She didn't say much, but later she would write me notes of encouragement.*

As for me, it was only when we passed over the wave-slapped California coast that the finality of our decision hit me—in a split-second of panic! I knew there was no turning back as I peered down from eight miles up at the Golden Gate Bridge majestically guarding the inner harbor of San Francisco Bay. A deep void opened in the pit of my stomach. I looked ahead at the miles of ocean stretching out before of us. Toward what? I wondered. Over and over, the same thoughts cycled through my mind: What had we gotten ourselves into? We had left home under a cloud, and we could wind up dragging ourselves back there in thirty days. Our confidence in our ability to hear God would be shattered. I kept all of this to myself; Donna had enough to deal with, and the kids were too excited for me to spoil their fun.

Hours later, on the short flight from Honolulu, we began our final descent into Kona. In the gathering dusk, I glimpsed the Big Island of Hawaii for the first time. What would we land on? All I could see was black lava rubble flashing by; it looked like the surface of the moon![1] Finally, we set down on the runway with a satisfying thump and taxied in to the prettiest little airport in the world, a lush oasis amid a harsh and barren moonscape of jagged volcanic rock. There were no huge buildings, just two or three gazebos surrounded by waving palm trees that seemed to whisper, "Welcome to the Land of Aloha!"

As we trudged down the airliner's steps, we were struck by a blast of warm, tropical air. We knew at once that we had entered a new world. Young Peter let out a whoop, took off his sandals, and flung them in the air. One of them disappeared, never to be seen again.

---

1. In the 1960s, astronauts actually used this island to familiarize themselves with the lunar surface.

Laurie remembers: *When we landed on the Big Island, all I could see was lava rock. Where were the beaches? I wondered. We were all very tired but also excited. I loved the Kona airport, all outdoors, and the smell of the plumeria blossoms, palm trees swaying . . . okay! And we were going to be in Hawaii for six months!*

While we collected our luggage, Darlene Cunningham and some of her staff "aloha-ed" our family and the other YWAMers who had arrived on the same flight. They packed us into vans and drove us a short distance to the little town of Kailua-Kona. Our family of six was assigned a tiny room in the Hukilau Hotel, a room that could barely contain its twin beds. We quickly learned the real meaning of "four on the floor" as the kids happily slept on the little bit of carpet that was still visible. Tired beyond words, we all slept deeply to the sound of swishing palm fronds rustled by the balmy breezes of our new tropical home. The next morning we awoke to another pleasing sound: the rhythm of waves slapping against the seawall just outside our room. *Oh boy,* I thought, *this is the life!*

Michelle remembers: *During our short stay in the Hukilau Hotel, Julie read my diary, so I poked her with my pencil. To this day she claims the lead is still in her arm. Other than that, I remember bugs and geckos everywhere!*

After eating breakfast in a YWAM ministry café (simply named "The Restaurant"), we went for a walk along the seawall. That's when young Peter made his second impression on Kona— by falling off the ten-foot-high seawall! He narrowly missed some jagged rocks before he disappeared into some good-sized surf. I jumped in and fished him out. Other than a good soaking and a scare, he was little the worse for the experience.

We were then given an introductory briefing and a tour of the mission facilities by one of the children's schoolteachers. The tour consisted of visiting two rooms above a large warehouse in the industrial section of town—the Maranatha Room and the Bethel Room. These rooms would function as our dining room and classroom. This was a little surprising, seeing as we had been told several weeks earlier that the leaders were negotiating for the purchase of the Pacific Empress, a large hotel that had lain empty and neglected for eight years. But hey, if this was what missionary life was about, we could adjust. It wasn't long before we learned that the foremost attributes we needed were not Bible school or seminary degrees, Billy Graham's preaching ability, or honed spiritual gifts. Instead, some of the best traits of a good missionary were flexibility, teachability, and a servant's heart.

Donna was especially concerned about establishing a "nest," a place where we would live. We could not stay in the hotel for long, because that would be too expensive. Besides, there was no way Donna, the kids, and I could live on top of each other like that for six months. We needn't have worried—the leaders had plans for us that must have been for our welfare. But upon first hearing these plans, we weren't so sure! As it turned out, we were to pioneer a "camping" ministry.

That's how we came to be living under canvas on a Hawaiian bush farm, our home for the next three months. Unlike the cramped motel room, we had plenty of room—one large room, to be precise. The old, khaki army tent measured twelve by twenty-four feet, and it came complete with flow-through ventilation—when the flaps were rolled up. We grew to love that humble home, sort of.

Donna remembers: *Our house in Montreal had been so important to me. I had done everything to keep it color-coordinated and had only bought the best. We had four bedrooms and three bathrooms. Now we were down to one "room" and an outhouse, which we shared with several dozen other people!*

I did my best to fix up the tent, but every afternoon the rain came, and within a few weeks our brand-new suitcases were covered in mildew. We had to get old rugs to cover the floor of the tent so we wouldn't cut our feet on the lava rock. We used orange crates as side tables, and fruit boxes to store our clothes. The first night, I was looking up when I saw a long, blue, poisonous centipede run across the roof of the tent. I hate centipedes.

We didn't know it would be cold, so we didn't bring any warm sweaters. I wrote home and asked for someone to send them, but that was the worst thing I could have done, because my family said, "We told you not to go there, and now you need us to help you."

I remember walking down the path from the tent, crying and saying, "God, what is this all about?" He said, "I'm not training two of you; I'm training six of you. Trust me."

I used to complain to the Lord when we lived in our beautiful house that it would take all day to clean, when all I really wanted to do was spend more time with him. One day, as I was sweeping out our tent, God reminded me that now it only took five minutes to clean our home, leaving me with plenty of time for him.

Despite some of the downsides, the fiery ocean sunsets from our tent were amazing. I kept thinking that someday Jesus would return in a blaze of glory, and I just wanted to know that I had pleased him.

The total population of our little farm was sixty-three: five two-parent families in tents; one single mom and her little girl plus another single woman, who bunked in a toolshed; two dozen single guys, who lived in two other tents; and a staff family, who lived in the so-called farmhouse. Sometimes we were able to use their hot shower. We tried not to be jealous of the smaller families who were placed in condos, apartments, and houses down at sea level in Kailua-Kona. Later, we discovered that we were actually better off up at the farm. In town, all the other single women and small families were shoehorned into cramped and sweltering accommodations.

Laurie remembers: *I did not enjoy life on the farm. The tent, the toilets, the shower—talk about freak out! The tent flaps flew up in storms, and our beds got wet. The toilets (see Introduction!) helped me stay constipated a lot of the time—I was too afraid of doing the wrong thing in the wrong place! Some nights the lava rocks next to our tent got "watered," because the "legal" spot was too far away. At breakfast we had to make PBJs for lunch—sometimes the only jelly we had was mint jelly! There were few secrets up at the farm. Everybody could hear everyone else's business: our friend Jay Brohmer[2] playing his drum, the little boy next door getting in trouble, the single guys talking in their tent . . .*

Julie remembers: *I'll never forget what our first Hawaiian home looked and smelled like. It wasn't necessarily a bad smell, but it was humid, stuffy air you can only find in a great big army tent. Mom and Dad made it as homey as possible, and I thought it was fantastic—except for the toilet situation. Our tent happened to be the farthest from the outhouses. In the middle of the night, way up in the hills of Hawaii where there are wild pigs and who-knew-what-else running around, a twelve-year-old girl's imagination can run wild. I don't think I ever confessed this to anyone, but I never actually made it to the outhouse in the middle of the night. Let's just say the plants behind our tent flourished!*

Close to two hundred people had to get around to the various mission functions throughout the district of Kona at different times each day, so our leaders created an elaborate bus and van "schedule." With finances tight all around, it was nearly impossible for the three aging blue, orange, and red Volkswagen vans (fondly named Love, Joy, and Peace) to keep up with the complex schedule. The valiant vans broke down frequently, and more often than not we found ourselves waiting beside the road for a ride.

Fresh out of the business world, I found this to be an immense source of irritation. I often stood on the roadside muttering about the inefficiencies of the whole organization. This "waste of *my*

---

2. Jay (Judson) Brohmer became a famous aerial photographer, winning many awards for his aviation photos. Sadly, he was killed in July 2001 while in a US Air Force F-16 on a photography mission.

time" became a major problem for me until one day the Lord rebuked me with a simple question: "Peter, what are you doing to redeem that time you spend murmuring and complaining?" I knew enough about the sin of murmuring to know that I didn't want to wander around in a desert of self-pity for forty years like the Israelites did after escaping from Egypt. So I repented (I was learning fast!), and the Lord showed me how we could redeem that time by systematically praying for each member of our church back home in Montreal. Suddenly, those times that had been such an irritation became times of maintaining contact with some of our dearest friends through prayer.

Our food in Hawaii was . . . let's just say it was mostly "high carb," although we did have plenty of seafood. Trouble was, the seafood was of only one variety—marlin, a fish that is not in the same culinary category as tuna or mahi-mahi. The Kona coast is famed for being the blue marlin fishing capital of the world, and down on the dock we could buy this highly prized sport fish for eighteen cents a pound! For most of the next three months, we dined on deep fried marlin, marlin con carne, sweet and sour marlin, marlin enchiladas, marlin chop suey—the cooks' creativity knew no bounds (though I don't recall eating marlin burgers). The children were not amused; they knew no joy at mealtimes. After we had all consumed ten lifetimes' worth of the much-maligned fish, the boat skippers got wise—or so they thought—and jacked the price right up and out of our limited budget. A collective sigh of relief was heard throughout the camp.

Upon hearing some of the highlights of our exciting new life, Donna's dad put his own spin on events. His interpretation of what we were experiencing was about 180 degrees different from what we were trying to communicate. Though we felt we had painted a positive picture, he became agitated that his kids—and grandchildren—were living in a tent while others (so he imagined) lounged in the comfort of houses and apartments. He felt it wasn't fair, and he was determined to do something about it. Just after Christmas, he and Donna's mom came to visit, along with

Marney (Donna's oldest sister) and her husband, John. Much to our embarrassment, Dad insisted on checking out the accounting practices of the mission during his stay. Evidently, the accountant was able to satisfy his questions, because we never heard another word about it.

Once our training school and the children's school began, we all settled into a routine. Then again, "routine" is probably not the best word to describe any aspect of our first few months in Kona. Surprising, unexpected, out of the ordinary, exciting, on the edge—these phrases go a bit further in describing what our life as missionary trainees was like. But as difficult as some parts of this life were, we loved it. Change was definitely here to stay. My own father had thrived on change. Now I was discovering the attraction firsthand. For years, I—like most people—had resisted change, opting for the familiar. The familiar is comforting and predictable. Then I thought of Jesus—no two days of sameness in his life. I was beginning to think this might also be true of us.

— Chapter 6 —

Back to School

Our missions training program, labeled a School of Evangelism (SOE), consisted of seventy-six would-be missionaries from several nations. Ours was YWAM's first big intake of larger families. The leaders made little or no distinction according to age, marital status, or number of children. We were all lumped in together. Classes ran all morning and most evenings. During the afternoon, each student was required to put in two hours of work duty. I, along with John Cardenas, a young man from Guam, hauled trash to the dump on a flatbed truck.[1] Our work duty was hot and dirty. When we were done for the day, John and I were in sore need of a (cold) shower to wash away the grimy sweat.

Every Saturday night, staff, students, and their children celebrated the approaching Sunday with a Love Feast, the best meal

1. I kidded John about whether he was Guamese or Guamanian—the latter is correct. John married a German missionary, Doro, and served in Hong Kong and China for many years. We visited them and their children in the northern Chinese city of Dalian in 1986. Tragically, Doro died of cancer a few years later. Serving as a missionary guarantees no exemptions from the adversities of life. It may even add some.

of the week. This was followed by a time of worship and special events, like dramas and musical presentations. These banquets took a lot of extra work, but they were the highlight of the week and set a great tone for the Lord's Day. Darlene Cunningham and other leaders had introduced them into the mission several years earlier.[2]

Our first teacher was Reona Peterson (now Joly). She deepened our understanding of intercession—a practice to which Paul Hawkins had introduced us just seven weeks earlier. We learned that consistently listening for and obeying God's voice should be a way of life for every believer. As we started praying daily for individuals and the nations of the world, we began to see a lot of fruit.

First thing each morning, we would gather together in groups of six to ask the Lord what nation or special thing was on his heart that day. One such morning, just two weeks after we arrived in Kona, Donna and I joined our respective prayer groups with heavy hearts. We had just received a letter from Joycie, who, along with her husband, Jimmie, was our close friend in Montreal. She informed us that the day we left for Hawaii, she had returned to her apartment in Montreal to discover a note from Jimmie saying he had left her for another woman. We were shocked beyond measure. Our kids were also devastated. Michelle was especially affected by the betrayal, as Jimmie was a favorite "uncle" of hers.

I shared this heartbreak with my group as we sat in a small circle on a nearby beach in the early morning sunshine. The Pacific Ocean lapped gently against the black volcanic rocks and pristine coral sand. In this beautiful setting, my prayer partners rallied around me and asked the Lord how to pray for this awful situation. There were many prayers of comfort and encouragement for Joycie, and prayers that Jimmie would hear from God

2. Evidently, early believers had made such events part of their lives as well (see Jude 12).

and return to his wife. Donna's group prayed along similar lines. One young woman felt the Lord say that Joycie was to move into our still vacant home and take in teenage girls who needed a mother's care and supervision. We immediately sent a letter to our church elders back home, sharing not only our grief but also this potential opportunity.[3] Before our letter even reached Montreal, Keith Price, an elder who had encouraged us when we were in the throes of leaving, telephoned with amazing news and an apologetic request. Joycie was moving into our house—as we were speaking—and would be taking in several teenage girls. Did we object?

Our sadness at Jimmie's fall was tempered with the joy of knowing that God had spoken to us thousands of miles away from the unfolding events. God said through the prophet Jeremiah, "Call to Me and I will answer you, and I will tell you great and mighty things, which you do not know" (Jeremiah 33:3). To us this was *a great and mighty thing,* and we surely hadn't known about the drama playing out in Montreal. Joycie stayed in our house for a year until the Lord led her elsewhere.

As school carried on, each week brought a new teacher with a new emphasis on Scripture, relating to tools that a missionary would need: relationships, character development, living with a clear conscience, spiritual warfare, and the character of God, to name a few. A highlight was when Corrie ten Boom gave us some of her principles of life, so simple and yet so powerful. Almost every teacher's teaching demanded a response to God. Where I had thought my life was in fair shape, I began to see that I had much to deal with. It was going to be a lifelong pursuit.

God started by working on the things I needed to fix with the person closest to me—Donna. Over the next three months I went through humbling repentance for things that had accumulated during our sixteen years of marriage. Just as mold grows on

3. Long distance telephone calls in 1976, especially from a remote island in the Pacific, were way beyond our limited budget.

bread, I had allowed layers of junk to grow on our relationship. This process was God's way of scraping and cutting it away. It was painful to my pride and painful for Donna to discover my hidden side. While she forgave me instantly, I knew that only the Lord, plus time, plus a change in my behavior would truly heal her emotional pain. I also learned that to keep mold from growing in the future, I had to deal with my bad attitudes, hurtful words, and harmful actions on a daily basis.

During this time, our finances were tight. One day the kids asked Donna for money to buy ice cream. We had given just about all we had for our school fees, so Donna replied wisely, "Kids, your mom and dad are being re-parented by our Heavenly Father. We're asking him to supply the rest of our school fees and our other daily needs from now on. Why don't you ask *him* for ice cream?" The kids did exactly that. The very next day, each of them received a letter in the mail from Donna's mother with one US dollar inside—earmarked specifically for ice cream! Through such experiences, all six of us were learning what Jesus meant when he told us to pray, "Give us today our daily bread." Jesus never said anything about ice cream, but for our kids it certainly did the trick!

One night Loren Cunningham taught on faith and finances. He entitled his message "Have You Ever Seen a Worried Bird?" based on Matthew 6:26. Afterward, we moved into a time of radical giving because there were many in the school who lacked the fees to cover the three months of lectures, let alone the three-month outreach that was to follow. Our family's ability to pay just one month of the required fees put us in a better position than most! Some of our classmates had been accepted to the school with no finances at all. As I prayed with Donna to see what we should do with what we had, which was less than ten dollars, God brought to our minds a young man from Australia named Peter Brownhill. He had paid nothing toward his fees. As ridiculous as it sounds, we both sensed we were to give him all that we had. We did just that. It seemed like a pittance that could not possibly help him in any significant way, but who were we to question God? Afterward, we prayed as a school for one another's needs and committed ourselves to believing together for all of our school fees to be covered.

The very next day we received a check in the mail from our home church in Montreal. We had no idea a check was coming— and that support has continued to arrive every single month for well over thirty years! Before long, both our fees and Peter Brown-hill's were paid off—and then some. Out of that $10 application of truth, we received a profound revelation about the power of giving, a subject that had always been ignored in our Christian experience. You could preach about anything except money![4]

The battle—for it was a *spiritual* battle—for the Pacific Empress Hotel was another learning highlight during our school. The leaders had made an offer of $1.8 million for the old, forty-five-acre property in the heart of Kona. It had lain forlorn and empty for eight long years. Well, not completely empty. Over time, squatters had moved in and claimed many of the one hundred rooms. She looked like anything but an Empress, but we loved her before we knew her.

One day the whole student body went to look at the four derelict buildings that made up the hotel. It was a sight that only visionaries and those who had been living in leaky army tents on the side of a cold mountain could love and appreciate. The hotel was in the middle of what had once been a nine-hole golf course but was now a sprawling mass of matted elephant grass inter-twined with seven-foot weedlike akoa trees. Rather than seeing broken-down housing surrounded by an overgrown wilderness, however, we were glimpsing the milk and honey of our Promised Land: a community home base from which to minister.

For almost three months the battle raged in prayer as we wrestled for possession of the hotel, which we had come to see as our inheritance, like the Israelites had.[5] The executors of the bankrupt hotel were asking for several million dollars more than

4. Interestingly, most of Jesus' parables were about money.
5. See Exodus 32:13.

the $1.8 million we had offered—an offer (as was reported to us later) that they had mocked. But we had the last laugh, because what they didn't know was that our $1.8 million was a *faith* offer. We didn't have one cent of it! We believed the Lord would supply the money when the time came. As the negotiations dragged on, the situation changed almost daily. One day we would receive a hopeful report; the next day things looked bleak.

After we had said grace for our lunch one afternoon (marlin? I don't remember), Paul Hawkins stood up and reported that, moments earlier, he had received a phone call from Loren Cunningham in Honolulu. Loren reported that another group, who had bid for the property to build condominiums, had just been given title to it. There were a few seconds of total silence. Then, in an act evidently orchestrated by the Holy Spirit, we rose and praised the Lord as though *we* had just acquired the hotel. The reaction was so improbable and dramatic that it seemed God was saying, "I'm more interested in your response than I am in any piece of property." Clearly, we had passed a test. But what did that mean, and where else could we settle in tiny, undeveloped Kona? It would be many months until the answer came.

Each Wednesday evening was "Big Family Night." Everybody—staff, students, children, and visitors—would gather for some kind of community event and a picnic. On one occasion I was asked to head up the games. Having just come from the Olympics in Montreal, it seemed appropriate to have a mock version of the Olympiad. We formed teams, each with a made-up country name, national anthem, and cheer. Medals were awarded for each event, ranging from the javelin (flinging drinking straws) to discus (tossing paper plates) to swimming (squirming ten yards across the grass) to diving (headfirst from a chair onto the ground). Needless to say, Big Family Nights were always a big hit.

There were also "Small Family Nights," when each family was encouraged to do something special together and possibly include a single person as well. Initially, our "big treat" on Small Family Nights (as voted by our kids) was McDonald's. The kids would find two-for-one coupons in the tourist magazines. Julie took the greatest delight in this feast. She always ordered a ninety-nine cent Big Mac. After we gave thanks, she would carefully open the Styrofoam box, take one bite of the burger, and tenderly put it back into its package and close it while she savored the mouthful. She would continue this process until she finished the entire burger. Incidentally, Julie was the first to be able to rattle off the ingredients of McDonald's Special Sauce—and can still do so today. With the coupons we could feed all six of us for three dollars plus drinks. As our financial situation improved, we moved up to Paniolo Pizza restaurant. And when our Wednesday Small Family Night moved on to Sizzlers Buffet, we thought we had reached the ultimate in fine dining.

In addition to fun times, we also experienced inconveniences. Having no car curtailed our independence considerably.[6] Sometimes the six of us were unable to get a ride to Kona Baptist Church on Sunday, a distance of seven miles. So we split into two groups of three and thumbed our way to the service. This didn't happen often, but we must have made quite a sight.

Once or twice on a Saturday, Donna and I left the kids in capable hands, laid aside our pride, and hitchhiked thirty miles through scorching lava fields to beautiful Hapuna Beach. It is set within a state park with manicured lawns, rustling palm trees, shady pavilions, and coral sand that is (usually) kissed gently by waves rolling in from the far reaches of the western Pacific. Those were memorable times, though they include one memory I would rather forget.

Donna and I were snorkeling in a secluded area just north of the beach, when a wave crashed over me and I lost my swimsuit! Panic set in. What should I do? My T-shirt would not get

6. This was after many years of taking such a mode of transportation as our God-given right!

me home in a modest manner. I could just imagine the head-lines in the local newspaper: "FOREIGN MISSIONARY CHARGED WITH INDECENCY." Salvation finally arrived in the form of our dear friends Uli and Carol Kortsch, who happened to be walking along the shoreline at that moment, and who just happened to have an extra pair of shorts with them. Needless to say, I have not been permitted to forget that incident.

Deep friendships were forming—friendships that continue to this day. Whenever a group goes through tough and demanding experiences, the ones who survive are bonded for life, like fox-hole buddies. This was definitely happening in our school. Later, we also discovered that some friendships are based on a common ministry or task, and when that assignment comes to an end, so does the friendship. This can happen in any Christian endeavor and is definitely a downside of missionary service. Jesus calls us to love him—and each other. But he never said anything about friendships ending.

The kids developed friendships through the fledgling King's Kids ministry, which Dale and Carol Kauffman were hatching at the time. Laurie, who was about to turn fifteen, was having a difficult time. The combination of leaving her friends back home, misdiagnosed eyesight problems, and the insecurities and complexities of being a teenager pushed her into a time of quiet rebellion. Young Pete, battling partial deafness (a birth injury), was showing signs of rejection, apparently stemming from hav-ing been given up for adoption by his birth mother. Despite our efforts to deal with his hidden affliction, it became a constant source of heartache and frustration for young Pete and our family as a whole.

Ultimately, though, we had the profound sense that for the first time the direction our lives were taking was pleasing to God. Jesus had commanded his disciples to "Follow me." We were con-fident we were doing that, but Jesus never said it would be easy.

Our thirty-day US visas were extended several times to lon-ger terms before we came to crunch time a few years later, when

US Immigration would say, "No more." In the meantime, as the school drew to a close just before Christmas 1976, we began to prepare for outreach—a time to put our classroom training into practice. Teams were formed and appointed to faraway places like Mexico and Samoa. In contrast, our family was put on a team that would stay and minister in the community of Kona. One of the main vehicles for our ministry would be King's Kids, who would sing and dance their way around the Big Island. Piece of cake, I thought.

How wrong I was! Our days and nights in the tent would prove to be heavenly compared to the four months that lay ahead. Outreach often takes people deep into unfamiliar territory and can be a disconcerting, stressful, and just plain difficult time. Tensions bring hidden issues to the surface, often boiling over and causing severe damage to relationships. My relationships with some of my colleagues would be sorely tested—relationships that I thought were becoming solid. Although lecture time was over, our training as missionaries and as a Christians was just beginning.

Chapter 7

Take Us Back to the Tent—Please!

With American Thanksgiving behind us, Christmas trees arriving on board air-conditioned containers, and carols playing in every public place, we eased into the outreach phase of our school. Perhaps "eased" is the wrong word. Our new residence, which was located next door to the construction site for a new Mormon temple, had been christened the "House of Barnabas." With a name like that, I thought we were in for some encouraging times.[1] But the next four months were not the most cheerful of times. In fact, we came to dub our abode the "House of Horrors."

Thirty-six of us were packed into the house, including eighteen of our little darlings. Laurie (fifteen) and Julie (twelve) were the oldest of the kids. As we shoehorned ourselves into the house, we were blissfully unaware of the challenges of living in close community. Very close community. The sort of community in which most of the world's people live. The sort of community

---

1. After all, Barnabas was an encourager (Acts 4:36).

that can so easily be the downfall of western missionaries, who discover that living in close proximity to one's fellow workers can be the toughest part of ministry. The apostle James said, "You can develop a healthy, robust community that lives right with God and enjoy its results *only* if you do the hard work of getting along with each other, treating each other with dignity and honor" (James 3:18, *The Message*). Easier said than done, James!

The House of Barnabas was a rambling structure set high on "Hamburger Hill," the local name for the section of town that stretched uphill, *mauka*, from the ever-popular McDonald's restaurant.[2] The house stretched out in several directions, with four detached bedrooms as well as bedrooms in the main part of the house. Donna and I were assigned "The Drum," so named because it was situated directly under a large living room area with a thin, wooden floor, upon which many little children played, jumped, screamed, and otherwise carried on. The Drum lived up to its name, reverberating unmelodically and repeatedly all day long. Laurie and Michelle shared one of the nearby detached bedrooms with two young women, one of whom, Mary Sampson, had recently been crowned Miss Guam. For Julie and young Pete, we squeezed bunk beds into a large closet in our room. To our surprise, they loved this arrangement.

Every community needs a leader, and ours was no different. The perfect leader is not only gifted to lead; he or she also must be a visionary, someone who can see the task ahead and rally the people to it. Leaders listen to God all the time and share what the Lord is saying with their followers. Leaders carry an enormous burden for the lost. Their gentle, shepherd's heart is so evident that followers feel needed and cared for. Teaching comes second nature to such leaders, and their model lives are always demonstrated by perfect order in their family life. In addition to all of

2. In the Hawaiian Islands, any direction away from the ocean is *mauka*. Toward the ocean is *makai*. To give directions parallel to the coastline, you refer to a town or district in that direction. This is an easy and sensible way of indicating directions when you live on an island.

these qualities, real leaders ooze compassion for people. Everyone considers such leaders close friends. Hospitality, wisdom, discernment, grace, and mercy flow from them constantly. Hard decisions are made in such a way that everyone embraces them as though they were spoken by King Solomon himself.

Nate Krupp, the leader of our outreach team, did not quite fit the above description. And I have news for you: neither does your leader. Yet this is what we all expect from our leaders—perfection. But only Jesus can lead like that. Human leaders, though gifted in some areas, are subject to human foibles and weaknesses. Sooner or later they will let you down, just as non-leaders also let people down.

Nate was a great guy and is a friend to this day. But he was mostly absent because of his call to go to Mexico for a good part of our outreach. Before leaving, he appointed four others—I was one—who would share the leadership duties, one week on, three weeks off. This seemed to be a wise decision, though privately I thought a wiser choice would have been for me to lead the entire time. In retrospect, it would have been far better if I had had no leadership responsibilities at all. Then again, it afforded God the opportunity to uproot still more sin in my life, starting with my pride.

Before Christmas, my job (or ministry) was with King's Kids. All four of our kids danced and sang with the troupe, which was an added incentive for me to be involved. I was the "front man," making the arrangements for Christmas performances at hotels and churches. I was also the soundman at the concerts, arriving at the hotel or church well ahead of the kids and setting up the equipment, then watching the program, and then frantically tearing down the apparatus and roaring off to the next concert, sometimes arriving barely before the kids.[3] Dale Kauffman, the

3. Lest anyone think too highly of my capabilities in this capacity, sound equipment in those days consisted of a couple of microphones, a tape deck, and a speaker. All I had to do was find an electrical outlet, plug the cord in, and set up the mics and speakers. I could carry all of the equipment in two hands. Today, you'd need a truck and a full sound team.

founder of King's Kids, coached and led the kids with help from choreographers, seamstresses, and others. Rod Wilson, a former hippie pastor, was Dale's creative advisor.

The King's Kids' final performance was slotted smack dab in the middle of the King Kamehameha Beach Hotel's Christmas Eve Lu'au. In the background would be a glistening white beach—beside the very rock upon which the first Christian missionaries had set foot in 1820, having sailed for six months from New England.

That afternoon Dale, Rod, and I were in a van behind the hotel praying for the evening's performance when we got into an altercation over a change they wanted to make in the program. I was stubborn and wouldn't budge on the issue. (I think I used my age seniority as an unspoken bargaining chip.) Graciously or ungraciously, they backed off, and the evening's performance went forward as planned. Silently my heart was saying, "Gotcha!" Pride ate away at all of my good intentions for harmonious relationships and team unity, creating a strong dislike within me for Dale and Rod. A dividing wall sprang up, and for the next few months I steered clear of them as much as I could.

To be honest, I saw Rod as a threat. He had intense eyes and a swarthy appearance—he was part Cherokee—and was what I imagined John the Baptist to look like. Rod had always irked me because of his passion to constantly be studying God's Word and garner everything he could from the teachers and leaders in our school. I thought he was a suck-up. Obviously, the problem was not his.

As we entered the new year, God continued to deal with such issues in my life, issues that I was certain I had buried, covered over, and even cremated, never to be dug up again. But God doesn't want us to bury or hide things; he wants us to live and walk in the light—his light. He wants us to be healed and set free from our past wrongdoings and bad attitudes. So, as I had done during our classroom phase, I entered into a period of painful exposure of my heart. First I came clean with God, who knew it all anyway, then with others who were affected by my sin. Once again, the "others" mostly included Donna. I off-loaded more of my "stuff"—not always with the most sensitivity, I might add. I was just anxious to be free of the guilt and to receive Donna's forgiveness. Naturally, Donna was hurt again, but a mixture of God's forgiveness and my new ability to walk in the light gradually brought healing to her as well. Silence and hiddenness make it impossible to be truly intimate. A life of openness and confession of sin when conviction comes opens the door to true intimacy.

Meanwhile, the House of Barnabas suffered under our roller-coaster of leadership styles. Dale Kauffman, Arnold Allen, Wil Turner, and me—you are unlikely to find four guys with such different leadership styles. One week it would be quiet and soothing as our appointed leader tried to bring peace and calm to the team. The next week would be bursting with vision, fire, brimstone, and a fifty-two-point agenda of all the things we were going to accomplish. Of course, the weeks I led were always perfect—in my eyes. In truth, I was a judgmental hypocrite oozing with pride. But I wasn't alone. All four leaders demonstrated huge insecurities. I fervently hope that during those days no one in the ministry kept a journal of our many quirks and quarrels.[4]

Besides me, other members of our family were still manifesting signs of trouble. Laurie was struggling with school and her self-image. Young Pete, now in school, was showing signs of not fitting in with the other kids. His experience showed me a pattern that I've noticed ever since: rejected people reject others.

---

4. Throughout its history in the mission, with one exception that I know of, the House of Barnabas seemed snake-bit when it came to its residents living as a contented community. The one exception, for which I humbly take credit, was in September 1980, when, as leader of a large school, I appointed Earl Pitts to be the student leader of the house. Earl's three-month tenure was a resounding success, and that was probably my most successful leadership decision ever! Earl went on to become an outstanding leader and teacher in YWAM and the whole body of Christ. Of course, I have to face up to the fact that he probably would have accomplished all of that without me in the picture.

Acceptance didn't come easy for Pete. And yet Donna and I felt, and still feel, that Pete was accepted into our family just as much as the three girls were. We didn't understand why he couldn't just be "normal," whatever that is.

Laurie remembers: *I can't say I enjoyed our time at the House of Barnabas. I remember lots of little kids, lots of noise, the bathroom being a bit of a hike, with almost forty people using two or three toilets. But thankfully they were flush toilets, and we could do all our "business" in one place! We also had a warm shower! I was not in a very good space during this time, though. A lot of the difficulties I faced were self-inflicted. I was making my own choices, and often they were not the right ones. My best memory from that period is playing Angels and Mortals one Christmas. It was a fun week, because after receiving anonymous gifts and notes from my angel all week, I discovered who my angel was—my dad, the best angel ever!*

Julie remembers: *When someone asks me what I remember the most about our time at the House of Barnabas, my mind immediately goes back to my "bedroom," which was actually a closet connected to my parents' room. And I didn't sleep there alone. I shared it with my little brother. For most twelve-year-old girls, the thought of sleeping in a very small space with your little brother isn't that appealing. But I didn't mind it one bit. Then again, I was quite a tomboy at the time.*

Another monumental memory during my time at the House of Barnabas was getting my first bra. I was not like some girls, who look forward to this milestone of womanhood. For me it was a dreadful experience. The box the bra came in is probably still where I left it—crammed into a hole between the sheetrock walls. I shoved it in there so there would be no evidence of this new season in my life!

Michelle remembers: *I had just turned nine, and I remember rooming with Laurie and "Miss Guam," Mary Sampson. We would sit on the stone wall and watch bulls fighting in a field out back. I also remember hitchhiking to church on Sundays; Dad falling out of a papaya tree and hurting himself quite badly; our first Christmas where we received only one Christmas gift each; performing in King's Kids during the Christmas holidays; eating pineapple until our tongues were sore; and last but not least, the House of Barnabas was the place where I threw up for the very last time!*

During our time at the House of Barnabas, finances were squeaky tight, and yet we never went hungry. To supplement our starchy fare, Rod Wilson's wife, Alexis, who "knew the territory" (when she was a hippie, she had actually lived in a tree house), would lead us up the mountain on "fruit runs." We tromped through abandoned plantations, looking for bananas, macadamia nuts, passion fruit, papayas, and best of all, mangoes. Alexis—an angel if ever there was one—taught us that we should tithe the scavenged fruit to others, no matter how much it pained us.

As our outreach drew to a close, I pondered what we had really accomplished for the kingdom of God. In many ways it was more "inreach" than outreach, for we had grappled with intricacies of our relationships. Jesus had prayed, "The goal is for all of them to become one heart and mind—just as you, Father, are in me and I in you, so they may be one heart and mind with us. Then the world might believe that you, in fact, sent me" (John 17:21, *The Message*). We may not have all come to one heart and mind for each other, but at least we knew what the cost was going to be if we tried. And perhaps, just perhaps, some lost person had observed our struggles and said to himself or herself, "They're a mess, but they're trying to get along." In fact, I do know that to be true of one woman, Mary Boyd, then the general manager of the Kona Lagoon Hotel in which King's Kids performed. She went on to join the ministry after an amazing conversion.

Let's just say our sojourn in the House of Barnabas was a learning experience. Little did we realize that around the corner—or up the mountain—another house, another group of people, and another phase of learning were all lying in wait.

— Chapter 8 —

Out of the Frying Pan

Mercifully, we survived our sentence to the House of Barnabas—for at times it did seem like a prison. In actual fact, the prison was of my own making. It was a spiritual prison from which I was being released bit by bit as I shed the shackles that had been binding me for so many years. When the time came to move out, I was a different person than the one who had moved in four months earlier. God continued the process of preparing me for service—preparation that has continued throughout my life, because it is really preparation for eternity. But pride still reared its ugly face through me. My problem was not with the leaders who presided over the ministry but with the people who worked alongside me. I had a blind spot. I was older than most and, therefore, felt I was wiser. Couldn't they see that?

Well before Christmas, Loren Cunningham had asked Donna and I to pray about staffing a Discipleship Training School (DTS) with Dave Gustaveson, one of the leaders in our initial school. "Dave G" was one of the most eligible bachelors around. He had tented at the farm with us, providing leadership for all the single guys. He was a good leader, and I counted it an honor to be asked to serve with him. When Loren gave his invitation, I puffed up a little with pride, confiding in Donna that, together with Dave, we would make a good team. But it wasn't a completely done deal. During our stint at the House of Barnabas, Dave had been off in California attending to some personal business (a matter of the heart), and it had blown up. It was devastating for him, and it took a lot of prayer and a personal visit from Loren to encourage Dave to return and lead the DTS.

The school would take place in a newly purchased house up the mountain, named King's Mansion. This was the first property YWAM bought in all of Asia and the Pacific. King's had been a large family home built by Henry Greenwell, an early settler from Britain to Hawaii, years after the first missionaries landed in Kona in 1820. It was easily one of the most beautiful properties on the Big Island, surrounded by lush green lawns and all manner of tropical plants, trees, and flowers. The mansion itself was painted white with a forest-green trim and had a lanai across the front that offered a scenic view of the vast Pacific Ocean. Even so, it took a bit of vision to see how more than seventy students could fit into it for three months.

The school was set to start at the end of March 1977, the same time we were to move out of Barnabas. Two weeks before our starting date, Dave had still not arrived back in Kona. So Donna and I were summoned to a prayer and planning meeting with Alan Williams, one of the four base elders, who would fill in for Dave until he arrived. We stepped confidently into the meeting room, expecting to meet with Alan alone. To my shock, sitting there with Alan were Rod and Alexis Wilson and Dale and Carol Kauffman. Loren had asked them to staff the DTS as well! I couldn't believe it. I could see right away that this was going to be a challenging three months because both Rod and Dale had very strong personalities.

When Dave finally arrived, he quickly gathered himself and made ready for the task ahead. This consisted of preparing places for the seventy-plus students that were about to descend upon us and ensuring that all was ready—not the least of which was organizing the staff to present some sort of unified front to these incoming students.

God worked in our hearts before and throughout the school.[1] The result was one of the best schools in which Donna and I have ever had the privilege of participating. Though the housing situation was desperate, finances were in short supply, rats roamed freely, and we faced problems and challenges of all kinds, God came through in a big way. Many of those students went on to become long-term missionaries, with some serving to this day. God also came through for Dave. One of the students, Debbie Christesson, was soon to become his wife.

In the midst of it all, our kids thrived (more or less) in the International Christian School (ICS), which was an integral part of our missionary "base."[2] Missionary teachers for our children, like all other missionaries, were in short supply. Jesus was definitely prophesying when he said, "The harvest is plentiful, but the laborers are few" (Luke 10:2). Paul Hawkins, a former high school teacher, was by then the principal of ICS. He did a valiant job of recruiting and keeping volunteer teachers. Like all YWAM staff worldwide—from the founder to the greenest recruit—no teacher received a salary. All were responsible to "pray in" their finances, trusting that God would supply. There seemed to be a

1. He had to work overtime in my heart, and my attitude toward Rod and Dale began to change. I learned that disunity among our staff would soon be evident to the students and would translate into poor relationships in the student body. Psalm 133 tells us how unity flows downward from leadership. Rod is now home with Jesus, but for many years he and Dale were my close friends. You might say we were "forced" into good relationships. Had we not reconciled, I cannot imagine how deep the negative effect would have been upon the students. I will say this: God has a good track record of producing good results despite our stupidity.

2. Up to that point, we were a base in name only. Ministry offices and our temporary homes were scattered up and down the Kona Coast. But we firmly believed that one day we would have a central home base, even though the deal for the old hotel had fallen through.

higher turnover of teachers than for most other positions. This kept all of our kids in some suspense from term to term, if not from week to week. Julie remembers that her happiest school days were when Paul (Hawkeye) Hawkins was principal.

If our family had gone from the frying pan into the fire when we moved into the House of Barnabas, the best that can be said for the move to our new home was that we hopped from one blazing log to another. Donna and I were put in sole command of all the student families with children in a rented house named Queen's Mansion, so called because it had once belonged to Hawaiian royalty. Only seven short months before, we had been in the same place as these families—freshly called by God, excited about serving him in some new capacity, challenged by living cheek by jowl with other families, and generally feeling pretty insecure by all that was strange and new. We still weren't all that secure ourselves, but at least we were getting to know the ropes. We also had one bedroom with a divider, plus a bathroom, which afforded our family some privacy.

Laurie remembers: *I still wasn't in the right space attitude-wise at Queen's Mansion. The six of us were crammed into a very small, partitioned room. The four of us kids were in two bunk beds just a few feet apart. During that time, all I wanted to do was sleep. School was getting more and more difficult and frustrating for me. And there were so many people at our place. I felt like I had no space for myself. But then, I had felt that way since the day we arrived in Kona. A good memory I have of Queen's is when one of the women had a baby. She delivered it right in their room. I loved babies. I would have paid to take care of them. Having a newborn in the house and the excitement of her being born right there was amazing for me. Years before we moved to Kona, I learned I could talk to babies and share exactly how I felt, and they would not talk back or judge me. They would just listen and love me right back—unconditionally. I loved being a nanny for different families. Back in Montreal I remember being paid twenty-five cents an hour and loving every minute of it.*

Michelle remembers: *One of the families we lived with fed their kids real tiger's milk. They were health fanatics. Then one of the dads who lived in a room below had his toenail bitten off by a rat. I also remember the night in 1977 before we left to go back to Canada for a visit; I was so excited I didn't sleep the entire night.*

Dave directed the school from his strengths: he was visionary, motivational, and consistent. He, Dale Kauffman, Rod Wilson, and I provided most of the decision-making leadership for the DTS, seeking the Lord before many sessions as to the subject to be presented.[3] Donna, Carol Kauffman, and Alexis Wilson mainly served in hospitality and the kitchen. We men were learning and have since become much more gender sensitive when forming leadership teams.

Though I couldn't discern it at the time, Donna is a more black-and-white person than I am, and can cut through most issues, seeing them for what they are and speaking truth into them. This gift—for it is a gift from God—is not always comfortable to be around for someone like me. At the time, Donna's absence from those leadership meetings was somewhat of a relief to me. Even so, stirrings of my conscience were pointing to another sin in my life—the sin of independence. Despite pushing them away, these stirrings grew for almost two years before I acknowledged them and repented to God and others. Donna, for her part, never complained about her role and entered into the lives of the students with her natural gift of compassionate listening and counseling.

Midway through the school, Rod and Alexis announced that God was leading them to pioneer a base in Kenya. Several of the students felt led to join them. One evening toward the end of the school, we had a giving and commissioning time for them. As each individual asked God if and how much he or she was to give,

3. We had this flexibility because much of the teaching was done with video.

I was stymied, because I knew we had nothing to give. Well, almost nothing. Unknown to me, Donna was having a mighty wrestling match with God. She felt him asking her to give her watch to Alexis—the very same diamond-encrusted watch for which I had made the insurance claim. It was very special to Donna, so she thought it could not be God asking her to give it away. But finally, pretty sure that it *was* God speaking to her, she leaned over with tears in her eyes and told me. My response was both disappointing and confirming to her. I said if that was what the Lord was saying, she should do it. Later, she told me she had secretly hoped I would say, "No, you can't! It was my gift to you." But I didn't, so she went straight to Alexis and handed her the watch.[4] As Donna says, "I was not a cheerful giver—I cried for a day."

With the end of the three-month lecture phase fast approaching and with various outreaches set to go, we prepared to use our return tickets home to Canada before they expired. God had already extended our stay in Kona, and we sensed it was time to return home and report to our church. We had good scriptural precedent for doing this. After Paul and Barnabas's first missionary trip, which lasted less than a year, they returned to their home church of Antioch "to report all things that God had done with them" (Acts 14:27). We believed that God was calling us to become long-term workers with YWAM, and that we were to return to Kona in September to staff another school. But we wanted to pray about this with the elders of our church before making a final decision.

The flight from Hawaii to Vancouver was uneventful. But as our long, slender DC-8 took off from the Vancouver airport on

---

4. There is a postscript to this story. Years later someone came from Africa with a small box for Donna. Upon opening it, she was amazed to see her diamond watch with a little note attached: "Africa is no place for this. Love, Alexis." Donna seldom wore the watch after this, keeping it in a drawer most of the time. One day she looked for the watch, but it was gone, presumably stolen. By then, however, its hooks were out of her heart, so it was no great loss. Donna prays for that thief to this day.

a cloudless summer day and climbed toward our destinations of Toronto and, later, Montreal, I remember looking down at the beautiful mountains to the north of the city and sensing a quiet inner voice say, "One day you will be in ministry here." It seemed like the Lord, but at the same time it didn't sound reasonable, for we were in the process of making what we thought was a lifelong commitment to serve in Kona. I decided not to say anything to Donna. Only years later did I find out that she had received the same word from the Lord as she looked out her window on the opposite side of the big jet![5]

The rest of our summer in Canada was a pleasant break from the pressure-filled ten months we had experienced as rookie missionaries. We spent time with church and family, and though not all were in agreement with our decision to continue in missions, our church released us to follow the Lord in the way he seemed to be leading. They also decided to continue their regular monthly support.

Laurie remembers: *This is when I became a Christian, in the summer of 1977. For that first year in YWAM, I did not have a personal relationship with Jesus. In fact, I rebelled against making that decision. That summer I volunteered in the kitchen of a summer camp in Quebec. One night I went back to our bunkhouse and asked Jesus into my heart. It was dark in the room; everyone else was asleep. Then a bright light joined me in the room—I knew it was Jesus. When we went back to Kona, I continued to rebel and have a difficult time, but that is the night I truly started to follow Jesus.*

Just before our scheduled return to Hawaii, we received an exciting piece of news from Kona. Since the heart-breaking bombshell that someone else had purchased the Pacific Empress

---

5. God did call us out of Kona and to Vancouver, but it wouldn't be for another ten years. When God speaks about new direction in our lives, it is critical to know the timing of the change rather than to assume that the word is always for *right now.*

Hotel, some of us had put the vision of it out of our minds. But now it appeared that we had given up hope too soon. The condo developers who were planning to buy the old wreck of a hotel and its forty-five acres couldn't come up with the financing. The Empress was now in YWAM's hands! Loren and his leadership team still didn't have the money in place; the only thing they had to offer in payment was a piece of land in Minnesota, a gift from Jack Winter of Daystar Ministries. The bank accepted this as collateral and gave YWAM an interest-only loan until the ministry could secure an actual mortgage. This news electrified us, adding new sparks of anticipation as we prepared to journey back to Kona and move into the "Promised Land"!

— *Chapter 9* —

Settling In for the Long Haul

With the blessing of six-month visas, soon after we arrived back in Kona in early September 1977 we moved excitedly into our new home in Building Two of the old Pacific Empress Hotel. Our family was assigned three rooms, with one to be available for guests as needed. Soon our third room was needed all the time for visitors. Many people inside and outside YWAM had heard about the miraculous provision of the hotel and wanted to see it for themselves. Our staff and student population also grew rapidly. So the six of us gladly pulled back into our two adjoining rooms and started shaping them into our permanent home—for the next eleven years!

Being on the second floor, we were able to build a sleeping loft over the bathroom area of one room, with steep stairs up to the cramped space beneath the roof. Once at the top of the steps, Donna and I had to crawl on our hands and knees and roll over onto the mattress that served as our bed. The downstairs portion of our room became the general living area. Young Peter was the only one with a private bedroom. He slept in a similarly built loft in the next room, while the three girls slept below. All in all, it was a comfortable home, and we made improvements to it over the years, to the point where it was the envy of those who visited—except friends from home, who were horrified to find us living in such cramped quarters after abandoning our spacious home in Montreal.[1] Even though it was close quarters for the six of us, we still had far more living space than most people on planet Earth.

The day we moved in to "take the land," we all gathered in the shabby, palm-frond-festooned central Pavilion to thank God for his provision and to witness the handing over of the "key" to the land and its four hotel buildings. A Hawaiian-Japanese gentleman, representing the interests of those who were by now anxious to dispose of their white elephant, solemnly passed the symbolic key to Loren and said, "At first we thought your offer of $1.8 million was ridiculous. Today we see that your God wins." You can imagine the racket we made with shouts and whistles. It rattled the tin roof of the Pavilion.

With schools about to start, we had to work hard and fast to subdue the land (just as the Israelites had to conquer Canaan and rid it of all that was evil). Over the previous eight years, the tropical sun had done its job, enabling prodigious and unchecked growth of all the wrong kinds of vegetation to strangle the once-beautiful gardens. Although the Pacific Empress Hotel's golf course had just nine holes, it had been the only course on the west side of the Big Island. Because of the rocky lava terrain, twenty thousand truckloads of volcanic topsoil had been hauled in from forty miles away so that the greens and fairways could be

---

1. Please understand that I made none of the improvements. Every time I picked up a hammer or a screwdriver, my family mockingly called out, "Hey, Bill," after Bill Cosby, who was the ultimate klutz when it came to home improvement. It was our friend and neighbor Gene Hackett, a master finishing carpenter, who lovingly and creatively remodeled our rooms with solid doors, pine cupboards with cedar paneling, and a mini-kitchen with a broad counter to sit around. One of Gene's helpers was fourteen-year-old Mark West, an Australian who was in the same grade as Michelle. More on him later!

laid out. Even so, golfers were warned not to "take a divot." If you went much more than half an inch deep with the swing of your club head, you could strike rock and get a "stinger"—tingling shockwaves up and down your arm. Now the faded old Empress and her golf course were far from their glory days. Prospective golfers would be hard-pressed to find a fairway—much less their ball—amid the waist-high elephant grass.

Over the next three months, every afternoon and all day Saturday, every man, woman, and (most every) child laid hands to the work of chopping, cutting, digging, watering, cultivating, carpentering, painting, plumbing, and wiring. It was hard, sweaty work, but it made for excellent bonding time. Loren, Paul Hawkins, Alan Williams, and Dr. Bruce Thompson—the base elders—were out there painting, slashing, and window washing like the rest of us. We learned a lot about servant leadership in those days. Nobody was above pitching in and doing the dirtiest of jobs. And yet we all knew that the leaders had stacks of other things to do: administrating, teaching, running the schools, communicating with supporters, and counseling. Yet we all had a single purpose aside from taming the land and making it habitable: to prepare a place that would become a multiplier of missionaries who would go out into all of Asia and the Pacific region, and eventually to the entire world.

Upon first moving into the hotel, most of the plumbing did not work. The shower tubs in each room had been abused, and the wooden framework that supported them was so rotten that in a few cases they fell through to the floor below. So for several months we took cold showers outside by means of a hose slung over the branch of a plumeria tree. Clad in swimsuits, we would wash down while cars and neighbors passed by.

The toilets were in similarly bad condition. They all fed into a central underground tank, which quickly became overburdened and refused to accept any more of our offerings. Our kindly administrator Wally Wenge posted signs that proclaimed, "If it's yellow, let it mellow; if it's brown, flush it down." After some years of these difficulties, at great cost we were able to hook everything into the main town sewage system.

Our food, on a scale of one to ten, was somewhere between a one and a two, although on rare special occasions it clambered up to a five. It wasn't because we had bad cooks; in fact, Graham Kerr, the world renowned Galloping Gourmet, headed up our kitchen. It was because there was little or no support money coming in for the ministry as a whole or for us as individuals, and our base was digging itself deeper and deeper into debt. The leaders felt that we should go on a fast. Not a "water only" kind of fast, but a plain, uninteresting diet of lentils twice a day for three weeks. Twenty-one days! Enter the Galloping Gourmet! Graham concocted a very inexpensive lentil dish—immediately dubbed "The Manna Menu"—which always looked and tasted the same, but was filled with nourishment and all the good things we needed. Mealtimes were unrushed (the kids took longer than usual to finish their portions!), and there was ample time for good fellowship around the tables. We saved a lot of money, and we believe the Lord was pleased by our thriftiness and obedience.[2]

Two weeks after we had moved into the hotel, the volcano at Kilauea erupted. Even though this happened on the other side of the island, we were affected by the "vog" (volcanic fog) that hazed our skies and troubled our breathing. Leo Bracy was particularly interested in viewing the eruption up close. He and his wife, Marcella, had been backbones of support to YWAM for many years and had decided to join us for a season. Leo, who ran a plumbing company in California, took over a lot of the maintenance and all of the plumbing duties during the startup phase in our new property. He was also a private pilot, and he wanted to

2. I have to admit that I write about the Manna Menu with little authority. While Donna and our kids endured this season (and gained a new appreciation for the food we normally ate), I was on a ministry trip in Europe for the entire three weeks, enjoying (out of politeness, of course) such things as pasta in Italy, cheese fondue in Switzerland, bratwurst in Germany, and pannenkoeken in Holland. I was also in England, but will make no culinary comment.

see the erupting volcano from the air. Marcella demurred, so Leo invited Cassandra Ward, the leader of our hospitality ministry, to accompany him.

News that Leo and Cassandra were overdue came in to the Kona base. Prayer became the order of the day. The next morning wreckage was found, and a great murky mist of despondency settled over us. It choked our hearts just as the vog was clogging our lungs. Some even had a sense that we had been betrayed. How could God let this happen?

We don't know much about the flight. What we do know is that as they approached the area where the volcano was putting on its magnificent display of fire, the aircraft entered an area of low visibility—probably a mixture of cloud and vog. A more experienced pilot might have turned away upon encountering this dark and soupy mixture, where visual references to the ground were nonexistent. Without a natural horizon to cue his senses, and not being trained to fly by instruments alone, Leo probably fought to turn away but found himself in a steep diving spiral instead. The situation would have worsened quickly until he lost control and they crashed into the unforgiving lava rock below.

Marcella's and Cassandra's families bravely decided that the memorial service was to be a celebration of their loved ones' lives. While we all mourned the loss of two fine people, we knew they were far better off. "His loved ones are very precious to Him and He does not lightly let them die" (Ps. 116:15 LB). It was a sobering time for all as we paused in our headlong rush to consolidate and establish what was becoming our headquarters for Asia and the Pacific.

It was around this time that God gave Loren Cunningham the vision of a university for training missionaries—the Pacific and Asia Christian University (PACU). A decade later, this name morphed into University of the Nations (U of N), which more accurately reflected the scope of this ambitious and unique educational experiment. The concept was for nonformal training programs at potentially any and every YWAM base in the world to be linked in a truly global university. There would be seven colleges reflecting the "seven spheres of influence" in a society: Christian Ministries, Counseling and Health Care, Education, Communications, Humanities and International Studies, Science and Technology, and the Arts and Sports. The first university campus was established in Kona. The original four hotel buildings would be called "Village 1," with several more villages to be built on the remaining forty-five acres. The village concept was intended to give staff and students the feel of village life, the life in which the majority of people worldwide know and dwell.

But for the moment, we continued to beat back the jungle of weeds (a year-round chore in the tropics), repair and restore the buildings, run an ever-increasing variety of schools, and send fledgling missionaries into all parts of the world. Donna and I staffed some of the schools. She also joined in the new counseling ministry under the leadership of Dr. Bruce Thompson and his wife, Barbara, who was a nurse. At the Lord's bidding, Bruce, a New Zealander and one of our four base elders, had left his medical practice in order to treat the "whole person"—body, mind, and spirit—rather than just prescribing traditional "band-aid" solutions that only appeased the physical, and then usually only temporarily. Thus the Counseling and Health Care ministry was born.

We also heard talk of a new type of school that Loren was planning. Eventually named Crossroads DTS, it was designed to release middle-aged people into missions to help build and staff the new university. Loren envisioned a dozen or so people that he would teach and interact with daily in his office over a period of three months. Upon hearing this, I felt a stirring in my heart that Donna and I should offer to help with this new venture. I happened to be in Argentina at a World Cup outreach at the time, so I wrote a letter to Donna sharing with her what I believed to be guidance from the Lord. Before she got my letter, Donna had received the same instructions from the Lord, so she went to

Darlene Cunningham to offer our services.[3] We discovered that the Lord could speak the same thing to Donna and me whether we were in the same room or ten thousand miles apart.

In early October that year, the first Crossroads DTS, designed for those who were at a crossroads in their lives, was held. News of this innovative vehicle for training middle-aged and even retired people for missions had spread. Many who believed that opportunities for service had passed them by found a new lease on life. When we gathered for the first time, instead of a mere handful meeting in Loren's office, the number of people, including the staff that was needed to serve them, had swelled to almost one hundred gathering in the tin-roofed Pavilion.

Pioneering a work seems to invite crisis situations, both personal and corporate. For our family, the temporary nature of our visas gave us constant concern. Every few months we needed to renew them, and each time we sensed that the immigration authorities were losing patience with us. Why were we staying so long? And how were we doing so with no regular means of support? Evidently, we were considered to be a drain on the nation's finances, even though our support came from Canada and we were therefore contributing to the US economy!

In late 1980 the situation came to a head. All six of us were summoned to stand before an immigration judge in Honolulu and show cause why we should be permitted to stay in the United States. Sometimes "the law," as Mr. Bumble says in Charles Dickens's *Oliver Twist,* "is a ass."[4] But laws, however asinine they may appear, must be obeyed. We sought God to discern what our next steps should be.

---

3. Unbeknownst to us, God had already spoken to Loren that he was to ask us to help him with this new DTS. When Donna told Darlene Cunningham about her guidance, Darlene responded, "God told Loren the same thing a few days ago!"

4. Mr. Bumble must have failed in English grammar.

An amazing groundswell of prayer and support throughout the churches in Kona produced a petition, signed by hundreds, requesting that we be granted a more permanent status in the country. When that failed to work, someone who knew US Senator Nancy Kassebaum of Kansas called to see if she could do something for us. Kindly, Senator Kassebaum called Hawaii Senator Sparky Matsunaga, who agreed to sponsor a private bill in the Senate that would delay action to remove us from the country. Deliverance! There was just one condition: Donna's older sister Marney, who had lived many years in the States but had never taken out citizenship, would have to do so and sponsor our family for green cards. Marney was willing to do this, and on that basis the Department of Immigration called off their dogs.

The irony in all this was that after eight years of fighting to stay in the United States and then finally receiving our coveted green cards, it wasn't long before the Lord asked us to move back to Canada. We now see that this struggle was part of our training. It taught us perseverance, to stand firm against all odds, realizing our fight was not with governments or policies but against spiritual forces aligned against those who seek to live out God's will for their lives.

In early 1981 we faced a corporate ministry crisis in Kona. Until that point, more than three years after we had taken possession of the Empress Hotel, we had been able to pay interest only on the bank loan we had used to purchase the property. Despite every possible effort (including continual prayer), the Minnesota property we had used as collateral would not sell, leaving us unable to pay down the debt and obtain a regular mortgage. Over those years, we all gave personally in offerings—often pocket-emptying and hilarious times of generosity. But times were tough. We had trouble just buying food for the hundreds who were now on staff as well as the many students who showed up with little or none of their fees. We didn't like to turn anyone away, and gradually we slid deeper into debt—the bane, and too often the death knell, of so many individuals and ministries. We owed $100,000 to local suppliers of food and other necessities. When our bank saw this, they dropped a bomb: "That's it. No possible mortgage and no further extensions. Pay off the debt by July 15 or we foreclose."

This left us with six months to discharge the debt and find a mortgage, or lose the property. Each giving what he or she could, with belt-tightening and other cost-saving measures in place, we paid off the $100,000 in the incredibly short time of three months. Thinking the bank might extend mercy because of our diligence, we were shocked when they insisted that we still move out by July 15 unless we got a mortgage from another bank. That put some fear into the camp. But generally there was an expectancy that God would come through. After all, he had led us to the property in the first place, and even though we had fallen short financially, God saw that we had repentant hearts.

As July approached, the Minnesota property still had not sold, despite worldwide efforts. No financial institution was willing to take a risk on a bunch of people who didn't have a very good fiscal record and whose philosophy was "God will provide."

New Zealanders David and Dale Garratt, founders of Scripture in Song and pioneers in contemporary praise and worship music, happened to be taking a holiday in Kona a short time before the July 15 foreclosure deadline. Full of faith, they felt the Lord telling them to make a permanent testimony of what was about to happen so that it would be a witness to others. They offered to make a live recording of our staff and student body praising and worshiping God, just three or four days before the bank expected us to move out. It was just like what King Jehoshaphat had done when faced with an overwhelming challenge. Knowing that the battle was not his but the Lord's, he appointed "those who sang to the LORD and those who praised Him" to go out ahead of the army. As a result, the enemy collapsed in on themselves. "Give thanks to the LORD, for His lovingkindness is everlasting," they sang (2 Chron. 20:21).

We accepted the Garratt's proposal gladly, and they began preparations. This included flying four skilled musicians in from the mainland, assembling the required recording equipment, and preparing and scoring all the songs we would sing. Altogether this was a huge investment for them, one that they shouldered entirely. Their enthusiasm for this project encouraged our faith even more, though perhaps some felt that this would be like filming the Titanic as it plunged to its watery grave! The live recording sessions were spread over three days, with all who wanted to participate welcome to join the choir. Set up in our open-sided Pavilion, with its acoustically challenging tin roof, the event was appropriately titled "Call to War." There were enough songs to make it a double album.

Three days later, the axe was set to fall unless a mortgage was forthcoming. Several events were planned for that day, all of a celebratory nature. King's Kids and all of the children were fully involved. There would be a big brunch, followed later in the day with a bountiful banquet. The night before, everyone—from youngest to oldest—slept in the field outside. It was our signal to God that no matter what, we would continue to serve him.

On D-day, as we finished the "mother of all banquets," Wally Wenge, our administrator, received a call from the Bank of Hawaii. Yes! They would give us a mortgage! God had seen our hearts as well as our outward actions, and he had come through. But he did more. Two days later we were given title to a twenty-five-acre property called Makapala, sixty-five miles to the north. It was a gift from a Lutheran ministry and was to be used for youth work. This was truly a bonus from the Lord!

With the crisis averted—for the time being, anyway—life continued on. Our kids were growing up fast. For the most part, they loved the community lifestyle, though Donna and I had some regrets that team sports, opportunities to learn to play musical instruments, as well as other cultural activities were not readily available for our children.

Such deficiencies were made up for by new opportunities, such as the chance to get involved in the unique Island culture. Upon arriving in Hawaii, we had assumed that the Island people and their ways would be just the same as the rest of the United States or Canada. Wrong! Like many Westerners before us, we had come barging in to the islands with a "We're here—aren't you blessed?" attitude. Jesus had indeed sent us, but we had never been invited nor properly welcomed. Eventually, we realized this and started on the long adventure of discovery that there are other cultures with other ways of doing things—sometimes even better ways.

One example concerned the matter of protocol. Westerners tend to be informal and casual. But in the Islands, welcoming visitors, giving and receiving gifts, and honoring the host people of the land and their customs are an integral part of life. Little wonder that there was some resentment toward us from the locals (the *Kama'aina*). Little by little, as we made more contact with the island's permanent residents, we grew in our sensitivity.

One of the people we became close with was Mary (Kamalele) Boyd, general manager of the Kona Lagoon Hotel. I had met her while setting up venues for the King's Kids' Christmas presentations during our first outreach back in 1976. Though not yet a believer, Mary extended grace to this *haole* (as we white people were known). Eventually, Mary, her husband (who later passed away), and her two children Gail and George, all came to faith and are still living for the Lord today. I had the great honor of baptizing the family in the Pacific Ocean (all except Mary's husband, whom we baptized from his wheelchair in the public swimming pool of the Kona Lagoon Hotel).

In 1982 Island Breeze, a team of Pacific Islanders led by Sosene and Becky Le'au, joined us in Kona and started to revolutionize campus culture. Their joy and laughter had a distinct impact on all of us. Their ministry was singing and dancing, a way of celebrating the culture of the Island peoples through the presentation of the gospel.

That summer, while we house-sat for some friends, we offered our two rooms to Island Breeze—though we continued to use them during the day. Five of the "Breezers" slept in the rooms, and soon our home became a drop-in center for the entire team. Thus began a beautiful relationship, which continues to this day. It has given us a deep appreciation and love for Islanders and their cultures.

Julie, newly graduated from high school, grew to especially love and appreciate the ways of these new friends. Eventually, she joined Island Breeze, not as a dancer, but in a serving role, helping with costume changes during performances and other duties. Had the Islanders not stayed in our home for those months, we might have missed out on much of the enrichment that has come to us from such close cross-cultural contact.

Financially, we had our ups and downs during those days, but God showed us even through the lean days that he was our Provider. One day at breakfast Donna announced that she did not even have the thirty-five cents needed for the coin-operated washing machine. Just then the phone rang. It was a local woman in whose home Donna was scheduled to teach a Bible study that morning. "Do you have any laundry to do?" she asked. "Why don't you bring it with you, and we'll stick it in the washer while we study?" Talk about an answer to prayer!

On a somewhat larger scale, back when the university was in its early stages, YWAM was also relaunching a ship ministry (several years earlier the ministry had had a false start). These two ministries—the university and the ship—were likened to the twins Jacob and Esau.[5] The ship, the M/V *Victoria* (soon to be renamed the *Anastasis*), lay stalled and at anchor in Venice, Italy, and would cost one million dollars to purchase, plus the cost of an overhaul. We already knew the cost of the university property upon which we lived—$1,800,000. It seemed that a lot of people who didn't have anything were throwing around a lot of big numbers! However, having *lived* through the whole hotel process, we knew we had a big God and that he had birthed both of these ministries.

5. See Genesis 25:19–26.

At a leaders' meeting, these "twins" came up as opportunities to which we, the leaders, could give. It was our custom that anytime we asked others to give, we would give first. We believed that as we gave, others would too. Each of us asked the Lord whether we should give, and if so, how much. Couples then compared notes. If they were in unity, good. If not, they went back to the Lord until they came to agreement. At this particular time, Donna and I had nothing to give in terms of ready money, but we still had the house back in Montreal. We asked the Lord if we should sell it and give the proceeds to these twin ministries. The Lord replied with a very clear yes.

As it turned out, the family that was renting the house wanted to buy it. When the dust settled from the sale, approximately $20,000 was left over. With no real sense of loss, we gave equally to the ship and to the university. Previously, we had thought that if we ever sold our house, it would be a nice little nest egg, something of a security in our old age. Now our security was completely in God's hands, but we couldn't think of a better place for it to be.

It's funny how some things are harder to part with than others. Giving the proceeds from the sale of the house was not a big struggle for us—after all, we remembered that back when our lives were being turned upside down at the Montreal Olympics, we had given up our rights to our house and other things we valued. But watches? Donna had had trouble letting her watch go to Africa with Alexis Wilson. And guess what? The hardest material item I ever gave up was also a watch that also went to Africa.

I was in Argentina at the World Cup Soccer Tournament outreach in 1978, and one night Joy Dawson, a well-known YWAM Bible teacher, spoke on "Giving and Generosity." Since I had no money, I sat through her message, nodding in agreement all the way through. Then came the application time. Joy instructed us to ask the Lord if there was anything—anything—that he would have us give away, and to whom we should give it. While everyone else was seeking the Lord, some even pulling money from their pockets, I smugly switched off, knowing that my wallet was empty. Then I sensed a warm feeling on my left wrist. It would not go away. It most certainly could not be the Lord suggesting that I give my beloved, perfect-time-keeping Seiko digital watch away, could it? This had been my company's expensive farewell gift to me (digital was a new thing back then). Because it gave perfect time—to the second—I became known for it, and pride had crept in. Being the custodian of accurate time was a large responsibility (so I believed), and God would certainly not want me to give up that dependable office of "official timekeeper." So I quietly silenced the enemy for giving me such ungodly thoughts and tried to dismiss the whole business from my mind.

But the business would not go away. After a fierce internal struggle, I surrendered and asked the Lord if he was asking me to give my watch to someone I knew. My friend Tim Bauer's name came to mind, and at last I had peace. Then and there, I took the watch off my wrist, found Tim, and gave it to him. Tim did not want to accept it; he knew what the watch meant to me, and he may also have been having his own trouble in receiving a gift. But by this time the watch was out of my heart, and Tim eventually accepted it. Nowadays I buy cheaper watches that maintain pretty good time and keep me from the pride of having perfect time!

— Chapter 10 —

My Big Fat Hang-ups

I had grown up without much in the way of worldly wealth. While a POW, I had only one or two changes of worn-out clothes, I ate food that was barely suitable for pigs, and I was sick with dysentery for an entire year. So having little in the way of material things did not make me feel insecure. My security problem was of another sort.

It all began right after Christmas 1945, when I was eleven, back "home" in England, and was sent to live for most of a year with a tyrannical uncle and his family. Finally, having despaired of ever knocking sense into me, my uncle returned me to my parents, who decided the best place for me was boarding school.[1] I was banished there at the age of thirteen. I should have counted

---

1. How a poor missionary family could afford to send me to an expensive boarding school is still a mystery to me. My dad never had ready cash, though God faithfully supplied his daily needs, and he did not come from a moneyed family. The theory that we kids came up with is that Mother, ever full of grace and truth, somehow managed to conceal from Dad that she had an inheritance.

myself lucky; many MKs went off to boarding school at an even more tender age.

My boarding school wasn't so bad, really. I was a so-so student, barely scraping by four years of secondary education, all the time dreaming of the day I would be free. If it hadn't been for sports—rugby and rowing occupied my mind and body most of my waking hours—my story might have been different. As soon as my final year was finished, I escaped England aboard the grand old ocean liner, the *Empress of Scotland.* Though the ship was pounded by mountainous waves in a raging North Atlantic storm, I was elated. I was on my way to Canada—my Promised Land—at the age of seventeen, set free from the restrictions of school and family and off to a new life of my own. Looking back, I see now how all of those factors worked together to build within me a sense of self-sufficiency, self-reliance, independence, and pride. I had fallen victim to the "Lone Ranger Syndrome," and I had it bad. Today, parents try to breed independence into their children as though it is the Holy Grail of success. It may be necessary in some aspects of life, but it's not a character-building quality. Lone Rangers are lonely rangers. Once in Canada, my solution for loneliness was to find a mate. I was a "marriage waiting to happen," certain that getting hitched would solve all of my problems. I had a long wait. A succession of girlfriends—each of whom I was certain was "the one"—slid by, until I met Donna.

I came into marriage truly loving Donna as much as I could. But, in fact, I had a totally distorted view of marriage. I thought it was all about having my needs met. And I had become so self-sufficient I didn't really need Donna to do very much. I could cook, sew, wash, iron, fly an airplane, control air traffic, and travel around the world. But there was one area where I was utterly helpless: intimacy. It was beyond me—and I was totally blind to this fault. Share my heart? Not likely. Disclosing matters of the heart was treated as a sign of weakness in my family, and I was ill-prepared to bring such a dynamic into our marriage. My way was to "tough it out" and "be a man." While I had felt free from the very beginning of our relationship to tell Donna that I *loved* her—often with a selfish motive—I had never said that I *needed* her. Deep down I didn't feel that I needed anyone, perhaps because I had spent much of my life not feeling valued or needed.

After almost twenty years of marriage, this problem continued to bubble beneath the surface whenever Donna challenged or confronted me. I don't recall the details, but one day Donna said something that was framed in her black-and-white, tell-it-like-it-is manner. I responded with my typical method of coping: withdrawing into my defensive I'll-show-*you*-by-my-silent-treatment attitude. But this time things were different. While never having enjoyed handing out the silent treatment, I had never examined why I dealt with Donna's confrontational style in this way. But with all the teaching we had been receiving and all our experiences in community living, I finally asked myself the $64 question: "Could *I* be the problem?" I didn't need writing on the wall or a voice from heaven to give me the answer.

Rattled by the revelation that I was not as "together" as I thought, I sought counsel with Dr. Bruce Thompson. Bruce prayed a simple prayer with me: that I would forsake the self-imposed isolation to which I had condemned myself and that I would gain understanding of my great need of others, especially Donna. Bruce also sensed that I had suffered rejection as a young boy when bundled off to boarding school. I repented of my pride and self-sufficiency and asked God to deliver me from this sinful habit. That was it. No confirming fireworks that my life had suddenly been put right. Just a quiet and deep understanding that I was embarking on a journey to overcome this deficiency that had kept those closest to me at an emotional arm's length. That journey continues to this day.

As I have walked this path, I have learned that there is a whole lot more attached to this "spirit of independence." This much-desired attribute is actually a trap devised in hell to widen relational gaps, increase misunderstandings, disrupt communication, and constantly cause friction among God's children. It is rooted in the deepest species of pride and releases all sorts of ungodly behavior. This includes manipulation and control, complaining, rejection, church splits, divorce, self-centeredness, immorality of the mind and body, and much, much more. Pride, through the sin of independence, had led me to assume the throne of my life, from which I attempted to control my destiny and relationships.[2]

Paul wrote to the Corinthian church about some who did not "[recognize] the body" (1 Cor. 11:29 NIV). He went on to say that the body of Christ is a unit, though it is made up of many parts, and no part—prominent or hidden—can ever say to another, "I don't need you." Having needs, recognizing them, being able to express them to others, and being able to meet the needs of others is what the body is all about. "But God has combined the members of the body and has given greater honor to the parts that lacked it, so that there should be no division in the body, but that its parts should have equal concern for each other. If one part suffers, every part suffers with it; if one part is honored, every part rejoices with it. Now you are the body of Christ, and each one of you is a part of it" (1 Cor. 12:24–27 NIV).

Pride comes hidden in a multitude of disguises. Humility—being known for who you *really* are—is a beautiful grace modeled by Jesus. It is the antidote for the sickness of pride. But there's a type of humility that is counterfeit, a pseudo-humility that expresses itself in the belittling of oneself, by downplaying the good gifts that God deposits in every human being. Saul exhibited this kind of false humility when he was to be anointed king of Israel. He had a low opinion of himself, even though he was

---

2. Oswald Chambers writes in *My Utmost for His Highest*, "The nature of sin is not immorality and wrongdoing, but the nature of self-realization which leads us to say, 'I am my own god.' This nature may exhibit itself in proper morality or in improper immorality, but it always has a common basis—my claim to my right to myself. When our Lord faced either people with all the forces of evil in them, or people who were clean-living, moral, and upright, He paid no attention to the moral degradation of one, nor any attention to the moral attainment of the other. He looked at something we do not see, namely, the nature of man" (see John 2:25).

"an impressive young man without equal among the Israelites—a head taller than any of the others" (1 Sam. 9:2 NIV) and had been chosen for this position by God. When Samuel went to anoint him, Saul hid himself among some baggage. Later, when King Saul blatantly disobeyed God, Samuel confronted him with his lack of self-worth: "You were once small in your own eyes" (15:17 NIV). Saul had overcompensated for his poor self-image by trying to overrule God.

In the midst of working through this issue, I received a letter from Bernie Ogilvy, then director of our mission in New Zealand. He invited me to teach in a DTS that he would be leading. My head swelled a bit at the offer. Though I had never taught in any kind of school before, I accepted the invitation and began preparing a series of messages. I felt certain that the launching of my international teaching ministry had arrived. I believed this was more than confirmed when Tom Hallas, our Australian director, asked me to extend my trip and spend a week with his school as well. I was on my way!

Donna and I decided that she should come along too. In my mind, I thought it would be nice for her to come Down Under with me (I had already been there once), meet some people, have tea with the ladies, do a little sightseeing, and maybe see a koala or a kangaroo. A lot more than sightseeing happened during that trip, however.

First, God was very gracious to the students in both schools despite my stumbling attempts at teaching. I think God must have bypassed my efforts and taught the young people directly. However, I was sufficiently encouraged to believe that the launching of my new ministry was a success and that now all I had to do was wait for the invitations to pour in. After I returned home, I waited. And waited. But nothing came. I had no idea how much I had come to covet such a position. Gradually, I realized that not only were my motives all wrong, but teaching is nowhere near my main ministry gift. But at that moment I thought I was God's gift to the vocation.

The second significant event while we were Down Under was that, at the request of the leaders, I reluctantly gave some of my teaching times over to Donna. God had been speaking to her about being a teacher. Donna had already told Loren that she felt the Lord saying she would be teaching, but she was afraid because in our denomination women were forbidden to teach in the church when men were present. Loren's succinct and wise reply was, "Get ready." And so she did.

Our journey was also the beginning of our love affair with the people of Australia. Never could we have imagined that we would return there so frequently over the ensuing years. Even more surprising was the fact that two of our daughters would eventually marry Aussies and that four of our grandchildren would emerge from The Great Southland of the Holy Spirit, as Dutch explorers named that huge antipodean continent of Australia.

As Donna prepared to teach and I waited fruitlessly for invitations to come pouring in, my resentment toward Donna started to build. It wasn't a deep theological issue that was troubling me. I had no problem receiving teaching from Corrie ten Boom, Joy Dawson, Darlene Cunningham, and other gifted women. Simply put, it was pride, the sort of embedded pride that said the man was supposed to be the recognized public figure. Although Donna's patience and perseverance in preparation, plus her personality and gifting, all made it clear that she was the one who was called to teach, it still did not sit well with me. As invitations started to flow in *for her,* I gave her little or no encouragement. It took several years for my pride to crumble.

The beginning of the end came unexpectedly on a visit, of all places, to our home church in Montreal.[3] Donna was asked to share

---

3. I say the *beginning* of the end because pride is not like a punctured balloon where all the air escapes dramatically and suddenly with a big bang the rubbery remains lie flat, emptied of all air. The puncturing of pride is more like the tire of a car that starts to go flat with a slow leak but you can still pump up again and go a few more miles before it needs further attention. The "end of the end" of pride will come for me on the day I am received into heaven.

on Saturday night after a potluck dinner, while I would speak at the Sunday morning service. Then the elders changed their minds and requested the order be reversed. "How dare they?" I fumed. But how could I refuse without revealing the pride in my heart? God dealt heavily with me all that week. When Saturday night came, I finally opened my heart and confessed the pride that lurked within.

Today, Donna is a favorite speaker in missionary training schools, women's retreats, *men's* retreats, churches, and camps. A word spoken over her during the second year of our journey in missions is true to this day: "Donna, you are like Deborah, a mother in Israel," said Alan Williams, one of our early leaders in Kona.[4] Indeed, today Donna is a mother to many people both inside and outside YWAM. The one subject that the Lord will not let her get away from teaching about is *listening to God*—the inherited right and daily duty of every follower of Jesus. I am now free to release Donna to do the will of God in any situation. We ask God together about every single invitation she receives, and we do not make a decision until we have total unity in the spirit.

I faced—and still face—more bits of ugliness in my life. Through these and other struggles, especially my struggle toward true intimacy with Donna, I have learned one important thing, and I will say it as an imperative: husbands, pray with your wife daily. Pray *for* her, yes, but also pray *with* her. In Ephesians 5:25–33, we husbands are told several times to love our wives. What's prayer got do with loving your wife? Everything! Just ask your wife if she feels loved when you pray with her. I like the way Eugene Peterson paraphrases Paul in one part of this passage: "Husbands, go all out in your love for your wives, exactly as Christ did for the church—a love marked by giving, not getting" (v. 25, *The Message*). Praying together is like a daily checkup on your relationship. Your prayers will bounce off the ceiling if either of you is harboring a grudge or unforgiveness or any other

---

4. See Judges 5:7.

of the "little foxes that spoil the vines" of your communion with each other (Song of Sol. 2:15 NKJV). Catch those little varmints before they destroy your entire vineyard.

As I battled things inwardly, our missionary base in Kona kept growing outwardly. Skilled volunteers from a group called Mission Builders joined us for a season and erected new buildings. Meanwhile, our staff and student populations rapidly outgrew every bit of accommodation that went up as the University of the Nations (formerly the Pacific and Asia Christian University) began to take shape. Donna and I were in a season of constant activity as we participated in schools and other ministries. And despite the challenges we were facing in our relationship, we were (and still are) on a journey, enjoying every minute of it.

Laurance Jordan (Peter's father)

Lunghwa internment camp (lining up for school)

The Jordans' home in Montreal

"Houses to Let Wanted" posting in The Montreal Gazette

Donna at new home in Kona, 1976

Pete at Kona airport, 1977

Shower in Kona

Fruit run (Carol and Uli Kortsch, Julie, Donna, and Pete)

The Jordan family, 1979

Pete and Charlie

International Council and Kona Leaders, 1980

House of Barnabas

King's Mansion

Michelle and Mark, 1989

Julie and Vae, 1990

Pete Jr. with niece and nephew, Rebekah and Daniel West

Grandpa and Grandma with eight grandchildren (before Ruthie)

Laurie, Pete, and Ruthie Worrall, 2010

Peter and Donna today

Chapter 11

The Classroom of Life

I had always struggled with school. My first recollections of education in a good missionary boarding school in China are primarily negative. Mostly I remember the consequences of my bad behavior, such as when I was rapped across the knuckles several times with the sharp edge of a ruler in front of my entire first grade class. That particular form of punishment, however, didn't have its desired effect on me. My conduct became even wilder, and I somewhat enjoyed the notoriety it brought.

When I was eight, the explosions that shook Pearl Harbor rocked the entire world. The might of the Japanese military swept across China and the rest of Asia like a tsunami. Believing that our family would be better off in England than face the turmoil that was brewing in China, my dad booked passage home while there was still time. My oldest brother, John, had already gone to Britain to join the Royal Air Force as a pilot.

Our ill-fated journey home began with two days crammed aboard a rust bucket of a ferry as it ploughed through choppy coastal waters toward Shanghai. There, we planned to transfer to a spacious ocean liner and cruise in steerage all the way home to Merrie Olde England.[1] England, however, was not so "merrie" just then. It was barely hanging on in a desperate battle for survival against German air raids.

When we disembarked at Shanghai's famous Bund, we were dirty from the unhygienic conditions and the smoke that belched out of the ship's coal-burning engines. But we were excited at the prospect of a long and slightly more pleasant sea voyage on our next ship. While staying with friends during what was supposed to be a brief stopover, we were informed that there would be no space for us aboard the ship to England. I think that Dad, who was somewhat naive to the ways of the world, got ripped off. Probably a bribe was offered and accepted, and our family was bumped. As a result, our brief layover in Shanghai turned into a three-and-one-half year imprisonment, surrounded by barbed wire and Japanese soldiers. It certainly didn't feel like it at the time, but the imprisonment just might have been our salvation. We heard rumors later on that the ocean liner on which we were supposed to travel had been sunk by Japanese torpedoes in the Straits of Malacca, near Singapore.

For the next four years, my formal schooling was interrupted. Eight years old, imprisoned, and a bit of a rascal, I posed a problem to sundry teachers, who happened to be in the same predicament as our family. Any attempts to get me to settle behind a desk and learn failed miserably. My actual education came through being a sort of street person, unmotivated by school but fully alive to all that was going on around me. Basic mathematics and other disciplines of the mind were foreign to me for those impressionable years. But just ask me about how to survive in tough times! In some ways my life was like the young boy in *Empire of the Sun*,

---

1. Those traveling steerage were housed in the bowels of the ship next to the anchor chain and steering mechanism. Steerage offered limited toilet facilities, no privacy, and poor food. Sort of like flying economy class today!

a film that was actually set in our prison camp. I must have been the despair of my parents, who had their own enormous challenges in addition to the stress of watching their kids grow up deprived of so much.[2]

When I finally did return to England at age eleven, I was placed in a regular school. Lacking most of the basics necessary for a secondary school education, I always seemed to be in catch-up mode—except that I was disinclined to play catch-up. The subjects that interested me were reading, geography, and English composition. These were subjects I had lived, subjects in which I was motivated. Thus, I scraped through high school driven only by dreams of immigrating to Canada, the broad country, strong and glorious and free! Free especially from the restraints of forced education! Or so I thought.

As I mentioned earlier, when I met Donna, her father "suggested" that getting a university degree would be a good idea. I understood what he really meant—no degree, no daughter. So I embarked on one more year in high school to sharpen up my grades. Then followed two futile years of university, in which I figured that phys ed would be the easiest course to take. Then I discovered flying through the Air Force University Reserve Training Plan. Soaring up into the wild blue yonder captured my heart (but delayed my hopes for marriage) and allowed me to discover that I *could* be disciplined and actually enjoy certain kinds of education. It took many more years for me to learn that if we turn the guidance of our lives over to a motivating God, he will

---

2. Dad would often get terribly painful boils under his arm and down his side, especially in hot weather. My mother developed breast cancer, and I had dysentery. For one year I was only able to eat dried bread and drink soymilk. Little medical help was available. Food was mostly a watery stew containing a couple chunks of potato and a leaf or two of some unknown vegetable. Occasionally we would find a small piece of horsemeat floating in the pot. But there was always rice. Not the kind of rice we see today, but dirty and unwashed rice that contained little tooth-breaking stones and also maggots. The stones we carefully removed; the maggots provided us with protein.

give us the desire to learn his ways and walk in whatever sphere he chooses for us, even if that means going back to school.

Even so, when Donna (a registered nurse) and I frequently found ourselves back in the mission's classroom as staff and then as leaders, I felt like an imposter, a fraud. God truly must have a sense of humor, I thought. Today, however, I understand that God is not as impressed with degrees and titles as with simple obedience. And simple obedience—out of love for him—was what we were learning. It is just a matter of doing the next thing that God asks you to do—the implication being that we have already done the *last* thing God has asked of us. And God's humor is further reflected in the title of this book: missions *will be* the last thing I ever do.

Obedience, true obedience, brings about a "glad to do it," "on the spot," and "done it" response. You have to have a willingness to obey God *before* he speaks. That is why understanding the character of God is vitally important: you have to know deep inside that he will do you no harm and that he knows what is best for you. "Everything God does is right—the trademark on all his works is love" (Ps. 145:17, *The Message*).

These and other life-lessons were the "meat" of those missionary training schools. Just because Donna and I were serving as staff or leaders, we were not exempt from continually learning and relearning the principles of living in good relationship with God and others. These schools were designed primarily to prepare people for the rigors of relationships on the mission field, though in actual fact they were training programs for Kingdom living in any vocation. Loren and the other leaders knew that the main cause of missionary failure is the inability to get along with coworkers. Culture shock, sickness, lack of support from home, inability to get a visa, and many other obstacles hinder missionaries from completing the task that God has given them. Success comes only when you "develop a healthy, robust community that lives right with God and enjoy its results only if you do the hard work of getting along with each other, treating each other with dignity and honor" (James 3:18, *The Message*). This is true for *all* followers of Jesus.

Our schools were a 24/7, live/learn environment. For three months in the lecture phase, we lived, we learned, we ate, we sweated, we cried, and we laughed together. Teaching was followed invariably by application of the just-learned truth so that we didn't merely accumulate head knowledge and not let it change us. As leaders and staff, we were learning and applying godly lessons right alongside the students. Many students had never seen a leader (or parent or teacher) humble themselves and admit to failure or weakness. How do you teach a person to be humble? Jesus is our main example; his whole life shouts humility! Moses—the humblest man on the whole earth during his time—is another.[3] Teachers or spiritual leaders can teach humility until they are blue in the face, but if their lives don't show it, the students will see right through the phoniness.

For those of us in leadership, it was paramount that we lived open and transparent lives before the students. Humility is the grace that opens the door to the heart. Humility is the willingness to let it all hang out, to admit failures, to allow others to see the real you, not just the side of you that looks good. Dirty laundry is bleached white when thrown into the washer of repentance.

I remember having to stand with three other guys before the entire base population—hundreds of staff and students—as we repented for taking part in a skit that made fun of one of the foundational values of our mission. It had all been very funny at the time, and there had been a lot of laughter. But once the skit was over, all four of us had a kind of sinking feeling in our spirits. It wasn't easy to stand there before all those people and confess that we had poked fun at God and made utter fools of ourselves in the process. *Walking in the light* with each other is essential for

3. See Numbers 12:3.

followers of Jesus. "If we walk in the light . . . we have fellowship with one another, and the blood of Jesus . . . cleanses us from all sin" (1 John 1:7 ESV).

At the beginning of a school we used to ask the "Four Quaker Questions":

1. Where did you live between the ages of six and twelve?

2. How was your home heated? Or, if you lived in a warm climate, when were you very cold and desperately needing to get warm?

3. From whom do you *first* remember receiving human warmth?

4. When did God become more than a word to you?

These simple-sounding questions can be very revealing. Once, as forty of us sat around in a large circle during the first week of school, a middle-aged woman was handed the microphone and asked to respond to the seemingly innocuous question, "Where did you live between the ages of six and twelve?" For almost ten minutes she sat holding the microphone, dissolving into a puddle of tears. The rest of us waited, some anxiously, some with compassion and patience, and some wishing she would just pass the microphone to the next person. But she didn't, and we waited until she regained enough composure to tell her story. Sobbing at first, and then gushing out in a torrent, her story flowed over us until there was not a dry eye in the room. From her earliest memory, she had lived in orphanages, a waif with no mother or father. She suffered physical abuse by matrons and sexual abuse by a janitor. Then, as she approached her teen years, she discovered the janitor's body hanging in a stairwell. She had never told anyone this story before. What happened on this day? Psychologists would call it catharsis. God calls it the start of healing. For the rest of us, it was a deep lesson about the need to walk in the light.

Such lessons did not just happen in the classroom. As with our initial school, each student (mothers of young children excepted) was assigned a two-hour work duty, be it food prep, gardening, secretarial work, or transportation. As a school ended, we gathered again to declare what God had done in our lives. I'll never forget what a veteran missionary-educator from Australia named Margaret McIntyre dryly recounted in her broad Aussie drawl. "Ya know," she started, with a twinkle in her eye, "God did his major work in me in the kitchen."

Instantly, all eighty of us perked up to hear what this great woman of God could have possibly garnered from working on vegetable prep. She continued, "The lectures were great, but I'd heard most of it before. What I learned was from these two." She pointed to her two kitchen teammates. One had been the director of women's prisons in a large and populous American state; the other an executive secretary to the president of a multinational corporation. Both had achieved great positions of authority in the business world. How had they had an effect upon this senior, lifelong, full-time-for-the-Lord stateswoman? Every eye was upon her as the answer came. "They insisted on teaching me *how* to dice carrots!" The room exploded in raucous laughter. We all knew what she was getting at. She had had to deal with her own attitudes right there in the kitchen. These two high-powered women kept showing her the "right" way to cut carrots, even though she had been dicing carrots her entire life! If left unchecked, such seemingly minor sandpapery skirmishes can eventually turn into major confrontations. But, thankfully, these women used the conflict as an opportunity to learn and grow instead.

Most of our lecturers came and taught for one week—about fifteen hours of classroom time plus one-on-one counseling, if requested. The thrust of the schools was to get "the messenger" ready to deliver "the message." Most messengers are not preachers or teachers in the classic sense. They preach and teach with their lives, not just with words and theology. Jesus modeled this for us with his disciples during his ministry years before releasing them into the world. Bible schools major in teaching the Bible and preparing ministers for the local church, but we majored in

life as Jesus meant it to be lived (on the mission field and elsewhere), with the Bible always as our foundational framework.
The schools dealt with a broad range of subjects, all centered
on the messenger's five key relationships: with God, others, the
Bible, the enemy, and the lost. As leaders, we had the freedom to
choose our speakers. Over the years, we developed deep relationships with many men and women of God who imparted to us that
which God had given them.

These schools were all about discipleship. For some who
attended, *discipline* had not been a major influence in their lives,
despite the fact that God had called them. Having to get up early,
take a regular quiet time, eat unfamiliar food, be on time for
classes, report for work duty, enjoy only limited free time, share
a room with others, obey "lights out" curfews—these were all
disciplines that would prepare a missionary for the rigors of life
in a mostly unfriendly world, in the mission field abroad or back
at home.

A few times we came close to sending a student home. Once,
early on in our school leadership experience, a middle-aged
woman made frequent and inappropriate advances to some of
the men, including me. The temptation was always to get rid
of someone who flaunted the rules of conduct. Either I was slow,
was afraid of confrontation, or had the patience of Job (probably
not the latter), but we did not dismiss the woman, and eventually
God met this woman at her point of need.

Another woman, who came from a radical feminist background, threw her lunch at one of our speakers after he used (in
her opinion) an inappropriate word: *lady* instead of *woman*. Our
staff felt she should be kicked out, for this was just one of many
misdemeanors. On this occasion, however, she repented deeply
for her actions, and we let her stay. She has gone on to serve the
Lord ever since.

There were others—mostly men—who we would have liked
to kick out! These poor souls were usually husbands who came
along for the ride, "suffering their wives" who were hungry to

grow spiritually. In almost twenty schools that we have led over the years, we actually did have to ask a middle-aged man to leave. In his former life he had been a teacher and then a policeman. He decided he would continue both of those "callings" in the school and became disruptive. Sadly, his big holdup was his refusal to forgive his mother, who had disciplined him harshly when he was twelve. And even more sadly, we heard that he later ended up in a hospital, where he again assumed his mantles of teacher and policeman.

With each passing school, Donna and I developed more and more relationships with YWAM alumni who had moved on to other endeavors. Eventually, we began to feel God calling us to stop leading schools and instead focus exclusively on alumni. That would come in a few years, but for the moment I was thankful that the word *school* had finally taken on a new and positive meaning for me. I realized that all of life is a classroom for those who are ready and willing to learn. And perhaps for the first time, I was both willing and ready.

— Chapter 12 —

Change Is Here to Stay

As our family had become more settled in Kona, God began to give me some rather unnerving guidance and direction. In my daily Bible readings, some verses jumped off the page and straight into my spirit: "As the eyes of servants look to the hand of their master . . ." (Ps. 123:2). "Better is he who is lightly esteemed and has a servant than he who honors himself and lacks bread" (Prov. 12:9). "He who cares for his master will be honored" (Prov. 27:18). "Then he [Elisha] arose and followed Elijah and ministered to him" (1 Kings 19:21). My New Testament reading was in Luke, and the illustration that Jesus used (17:7–10) to describe the role of a servant toward his master also touched my heart.

All this about serving was great, but who was *my* master? I got the impression that God was pointing me to Loren Cunningham. I knew Loren well enough to know that he would squirm if the term "master" were ever used to describe his position. He was the epitome of a servant leader, and yet I had this strong sense that I was to serve him, whatever that entailed.

But who was I to make such an offer? One of the reasons for my hesitation was that I had come from a business culture where jobs and positions were fought over in brutal wars as people sought to advance their careers. Now I was in a culture that encouraged exactly the opposite principles: humility, servanthood, and self-sacrifice. After sitting on this guidance for a few days, I finally shared it with Donna. She felt an immediate agreement in her spirit and told me to go for it. Plucking up my courage, I booked an appointment with Loren.

Upon entering his office, I swallowed my doubts and fears and took the plunge, telling him I felt the Lord was asking me to offer myself to serve him in any way I could. I held my breath as I waited for his response. What he said blew away what little breath remained. He told me that he and the three other council members had just been praying about asking me to join them in base leadership. Furthermore, he had an immediate need for my practical assistance.

Loren traveled a lot in ministry. Up to that point, each time he was away, one of the other three council members would take over Loren's duties in addition to their own work. This wasn't an ideal situation, seeing as the three council members all had such distinct personalities and giftings. (It was the same sort of challenge we had faced back in the House of Barnabas.) There was Paul Hawkins, the kind of man who sought God about everything. He treated everything that happened to him and others as merely another lesson in life. There was also Dr. Bruce Thompson. He was as kind, caring, and gentle as a Kona breeze. He possessed great discernment and a knack for putting everyone at ease. Finally, there was Alan Williams, a fiery little giant of a man who was an ex-lightweight boxer. Though he possessed a softer side, Alan was usually an in-your-face, back-down-from-nothing sort of guy. This made him a fearless evangelist, willing to tackle any situation with his whole heart. As you can imagine, it was not easy for the staff to adjust to such vastly differing leadership styles when Loren was away.

The next time Loren left on a ministry trip, he asked me to assume leadership of the base. I must have done an okay job, because for the next several years I filled that role every time Loren traveled. I was a maintainer for Loren, providing a measure of leadership consistency while he was away. It was not my job to get new vision for the base—a commodity never in short supply in YWAM! Nor was I to develop a leadership style of my own. I was merely to sustain and nurture those things God had already given to Loren and the council. As I look back, I am staggered at the trust and responsibility that was placed upon me. And yet I enjoyed a measure of comfort in that role, because I knew that God had called me into it. I was operating within the limits of my gifting, and that transmitted itself to the base population, who were generally content with my leadership style.[1] It has always amazed me how many people want to be leaders even though they are not strongly gifted that way. One of the keys to life that I have discovered is to be realistic about my strengths and weaknesses and to serve within my boundaries.

In his book *The Peter Principle,* Dr. Laurence J. Peter pointed out that in most organizations people tend to rise to their level of incompetence. That certainly became true for me. After leading several Crossroads Discipleship Training Schools, my service to Loren began to suffer. So Dean Sherman, a member of the base council and a much sought-after teacher, took over leadership of Crossroads. After two or three years away from schools, though, Dean was juggling four schools per year, with a new one starting every three months. He asked if Donna and I would lead one school a year. We were already feeling the itch to get back into

---

1. I am sure that not everyone liked my style. Leaders are targets not only of accolades but also of fusillades. The easiest part of a target to hit is its weakest and most vulnerable point. One of my shortcomings was my avoidance of any kind of confrontation. My attitude was "let sleeping dogs lie" or "time will take care of all problems." But a leader must confront some issues head-on. This was an area in which I was weak and vulnerable to plenty of justified criticism.

Crossroads, so we gladly agreed to take on the January to March schools during the mid- to late-1980s. These were rich years of relationships with both staff and students. Outreaches from these schools took us to Hong Kong, the Philippines, Thailand, South Korea, and to my homeland, China.

In early 1986 Donna and I sensed the Lord putting the desire in our hearts to take a pastoral journey through Asia so we could visit and encourage our far-flung staff throughout that hugely populated region. We also felt we were to take along fifteen-year-old Pete. Loren graciously wrote a letter to all of the Asian base leaders introducing and commending us and requesting that we be received. Then we planned a three-month itinerary based on a very flexible around-the-world airline routing (no longer so flexible!). We planned to start in Japan and crisscross Asia as far as Bombay. From there, we would continue westward until we reached Hawaii. In all of this, there was but one hitch: Donna's dad was sick with cancer and not expected to live many more months. She had just visited him, said her goodbyes, and perhaps more importantly, had finally received his blessing after living eight years in missions without that so-important approval. Over the years, her father had softened from his negative stance toward his daughter's foray into missions. But even though we left on schedule with a final confirmation from the Lord, Donna still agonized over departing on such a long journey with her father so sick.

Following a wonderful time with the staff in Japan, we moved on to Seoul. After teaching at a DTS very close to the DMZ (demilitarized zone) between North and South Korea,[2] Donna received a phone call informing her that her father had died. While she headed home for the funeral, Pete and I continued on to Taiwan and then the Philippines, where Donna caught up to us again. Next, we moved on to Hong Kong, China (where

2. So close that we could hear the huge and highly amplified loudspeakers that blasted Communist propaganda from the North night and day.

I was able to show Donna and Pete my birthplace), Indonesia, Singapore, and Thailand. We spent our three final weeks in India and Nepal.

Throughout the trip, Pete was a blessing to us. He had a great time taking in the exotic sights and unique experiences. These included "Snake Alley" in Taipei, long distance train rides in China and India, and a visit to Cambodian refugee camps in Thailand (where, much to his mother's disgust, Pete got to curl an enormous snake around his neck). He also savored the wonderful foods of the East, including a Philippine favorite called *balut*, "the egg with legs," so called because it is a chick on the verge of hatching. Pete told us the legs were a bit crunchy and the feathers stuck in his throat, but otherwise it was okay! He wasn't too impressed, though, with an Indian snake charmer who used his flute to rap his lazy cobra over the head to make it rise from the basket. A YWAMer from Nagaland was so impressed with the way Pete related to us that he gave him a special cape made in his region of India.

One night in the Philippines, the three of us were enjoying a late supper with Kel and Kristyn Steiner, the directors of YWAM Philippines. Kel, a veteran missionary of many years, had been one of YWAM's most eligible bachelors. He was finally won over by Kristyn, fifteen years his junior. Upon hearing of their age difference, fifteen-year-old Pete sat pensively for a while and then spoke up with a twinkle in his eye. "This is scary. Right now, somewhere in the world, there could be a brand-new baby who may become my wife one day!"

One of the valuable lessons we learned during those three months in Asia related to the use of the word *busy*. It's such a common expression, and we use it a lot, frequently with the implication, "I'm important, I don't have time for you." I discovered that the Chinese (and Japanese) character for "busy" has two parts, which separately mean "Heart-Dead." The word *busy* is no longer part of our vocabulary.

After we arrived back in Kona, Donna and I picked up where we left off, still deeply moved by the opportunity to fellowship with so many of our field workers. Throughout that journey, God had put a new desire in our hearts for visitation and encouragement. The very next year, he gave us a plan to go and see some of our former students and staff who were no longer with the mission. For eight weeks in July and August of 1987, we set out again, this time traveling to Washington State and British Columbia. Our old and dear friends Uli and Carol Kortsch loaned us their ancient, mustard-colored, propane-burning Volvo station wagon for the journey.[3]

For two months, we drove through some of the most beautiful, mountainous, and rugged scenery in the world, staying a day or two here and there with friends we had met in Kona. In the small city of Vernon, BC, we stayed with Don and Caroline Coleridge, who ran a thriving fruit juice business. As we reminisced about our Kona days, inevitably the names of others we knew in that region came up. So we made plans to return in a few days and have a BBQ picnic for all of the former YWAMers we could gather.

Word got around, and when we returned to Vernon, more than sixty people showed up for the picnic on a beautiful summer evening. After the meal, we sat around while Donna and I shared some of the latest news from Kona. Then we prayed for some who were going through difficult times and just enjoyed being together. As the sun went down behind the mountains and the air started to cool, we all agreed that we had to do this again. Something was stirring in our hearts. Donna understood what it was, but I didn't see it quite yet.

Soon afterward, we drove down to Tacoma, Washington, where we stayed for a few days with Graham and Treena Kerr.

---

3. Uli had always been a bit of a "green guy." Wherever he settled, he managed to convert fossil-fuel-burning furnaces to wood-burners. He always had enormous mounds of firewood in his backyard, which he split by hooking up some ingenious Rube Goldberg contraption to the rear axle of his car.

Neither of them was ever shy about voicing what they felt God was saying in any situation. It was an enjoyable visit. The food was magnificent, of course, but something was not sitting right with me as we talked about all these people we were visiting, many of whom were experiencing everything from mild discouragement to a crisis of faith. To Donna, it was clear: God was showing us that we were to make a "career" change, to devote ourselves full-time to a ministry of encouragement to all those who had served and then left the mission. Even though the need seemed great, my loyalty was still with Loren and the Kona base. After all, we were "lifers." Why would we ever leave Kona? And where would we set up this new ministry, anyway? Surely not outside the US after all the hassles we had gone through to get our green cards. It was the three of them against me, but I was stubborn, determined that God could not be changing his mind about the ministry to which he had directed us in the first place.

After a few nights of wrestling, however, God spoke to my spirit in that quiet voice, assuring me that what Donna and the Kerrs were hearing was right. This course change was his doing. At last, I surrendered my position and agreed with God. But I still wanted to know how and why this was to happen.

If I was honest with myself, I knew our ministry in Kona was changing, though we were still perfectly happy and content in being there. The base was evolving as new schools and degree-bearing instructors were added to the university. The whole environment was moving in an academic direction—and I had never been accused of being an academic! As founder and chancellor of the University of the Nations, Loren needed people around him who could provide this sort of academic input. Despite this line of reasoning, however, it all boiled down to whether or not I was willing to make this radical change. Obedience once again.

As Donna and I returned to Kona from that decisive ministry trip, we prayed that when we shared our new vision with the other leaders, especially Loren and Darlene, they would seek God about it and would have the same witness in their spirits. We wrote out a proposal and presented it to the Cunninghams and then waited anxiously for their response. Finally, after a couple of weeks, they invited us to lunch at a local hotel.

On a lanai that overlooked sloping green lawns stretching down to the seashore, we made small talk until we had finished our mahi mahi sandwiches and the plates were cleared. Only then did the moment for which we had waited so nervously arrive. Loren told us that before asking the Lord about our request, they had demurred at the very thought of us leaving. But the Lord had confirmed our vision to them. Furthermore, they wanted us to present our plans to the entire council. Soon afterward, we did exactly that. The council also confirmed our proposal, though several expressed sadness at the prospect of our departure. We felt the same way when we thought about leaving our close friends, with whom we had experienced so much.

Once the decision was made, it was time to figure out our next move. Where would we go? Then God reminded us of what he had told us on that flight out of Vancouver ten years earlier. Independently and simultaneously, Donna and I had heard the Lord say, "One day you will be in ministry here." A decade later, God confirmed that the timing was now right.

Truth be told, by 1987 we had pretty much forgotten about the idea of doing ministry in Vancouver. Those many years ago, we had hung that guidance on a hook, not fully understanding it and wondering if we had misheard God. Though we were Canadians, Vancouver was almost three thousand miles from where we had lived before YWAM, and we barely knew anyone there. Vancouver was a beautiful city, but it held no particular appeal. Nevertheless, we now looked to Vancouver to see what God would reveal to us.

By coincidence—or by divine intervention—I had to stop over in Vancouver that fall, on my way back from a ministry event in eastern Canada. My layover took place on a weekend, so I decided to go to church. While there, I ran into Dr. Carl Armerding, who was president of Regent College, a wonderful international graduate school of Christian studies. He and his wife, Betsy, were interested in talking to me about YWAM, and they invited me over for tea that evening.

The Armerdings were considering taking a sabbatical from Regent and living in Kona for a year. As I was answering their questions about the University of the Nations, the Lord's still, small voice whispered to me, "You will be living in this house while they are away."

Preposterous! No chance! You're dreaming! I thought. The rent alone for this beautiful home in one of the most exclusive parts of Vancouver was way beyond our means.

Just as I was processing—and rejecting—what I was hearing, the phone rang. It was Bill McAllister, Donna's second cousin and a dear friend whom we had met in Kona years before. I had been trying to connect with Bill and his wife, Jean, all weekend. My hope was that he would know a place where we might live when we moved to Vancouver the following spring.

I took the call in another room and told Bill briefly of our plans. When I asked him to be on the lookout for some suitable housing, he paused and said, "You will be living right there in the Armerdings' house."

What?

Reeling from Bill's outrageous confirmation of what the Lord had just spoken to me, I rejoined the Armerdings in their living room, where we continued our conversation about life in Kona. But God wasn't finished with me just yet.

As I got up to leave, Carl asked, "Would you and your wife consider renting our home while we're away?" I didn't know whether to jump up and down or act cool. A thousand things rushed through my mind at that moment, not the least of which was the question of the cost of renting in an exclusive part of Vancouver. Seeing the mix of emotions on my face, Carl continued quickly, "Oh yes, about rent, this is what we would need." He gave me a figure that was about one-third of the amount that the house could easily command! I returned to Kona the following day and shared the good news with Donna. It seemed like a no-brainer, but we asked the Lord about it anyway. He answered with a resounding "Yes!"

Our kids were now old enough to ask the Lord what he wanted them to do when we moved to Vancouver. As it turned out, all three girls felt they were to come with us. Laurie, still battling major health issues, would continue for a while as a dental assistant. Julie, who we all *knew* would marry an Islander, felt she should be with us in Vancouver and take a course in working with physically and mentally challenged children, even though this would mean going three thousand miles *away* from the Islands. Michelle believed she was to come with us too, though by now she was more and more firmly established in her relationship with a young man. Pete had just returned to Hawaii after leaving prematurely from a YWAM school. So he decided to stay behind in Honolulu.

During our final three months in Kona, we led the largest school ever held at the Kona base up to that point, with 105 students. It was a marvelous experience, but with our staff numbering only eight, it was also a stretching time for all. Some of our students were Elmer and Jean Darnall—Jean, a favorite teacher in YWAM—and Jimmy and Carol Owens, father and mother to many Christian musicians.

In addition to the constant demands of the school, Donna and I were packing up to leave permanently. Despite our simple lifestyle, over eleven years we had accumulated furniture, appliances, a car, and other odds and ends that would neither be appropriate nor convenient to haul to the west coast of Canada. We made a list of items we would not take with us and began to assign prices to each so we could sell them and raise enough money for our airfares home.

It so happened that during that time, the entire campus was living out "ten days of generosity." Everyone was encouraged to be generous in many ways, not just with finances, but also with time and possessions. During our family dinner one night, Donna said, "Since when do we sell to our brothers and sisters? Let's ask the Lord to show us who we should give things to, then give them all away." We had the greatest time going down our list of items that we would leave behind, asking the Lord, "Who's this for? Who should get that?"

When we had all of the items assigned, we dropped notes in the recipients' mailboxes, telling them to come and pick up their desk, their oven, their sofa, or whatever it happened to be. What fun! At a campus prayer time just days before we flew to Vancouver, several people wanted to express their thanks to the Lord. They jumped up and exclaimed things like, "Thank you, Lord for the fridge!" "I've been praying for a desk for weeks, and now I have one!" Donna and I smiled knowingly at each other. And wouldn't you know it? God supplied all of our airfares plus enough money to buy a car and other items so that we could get established in our new home.

And so our time in Hawaii came to an end. With a mixture of sadness and anticipation, we bid farewell to our many friends. But as the locals say, "You can take the boy out of the islands, but can't take the islands out of the boy." To this day, our twelve years in Hawaii have added richness and flavor to our lives. We aren't the same as when we first landed in Kona. Our time in Hawaii also prepared us for the changes that lay ahead. But what would those changes look like?

— *Chapter 13* —

Two Love Stories

We spent our first year in Canada living in Carl and Betsy Armerding's beautiful home in a classy neighborhood of Vancouver. For the first time in twelve years, our girls each had their own bedroom. It was a wonderful time as we joined a church community and got reacquainted with our homeland.

Donna and I even "inherited" Carl and Betsy's home fellowship group—a daunting experience if we ever had one! The rest of the group was made up of professors and their wives from Regent College, including Gordon and Maudine Fee, Eugene and Janice Peterson, Michael and Rosemary Green, Bruce and Elaine Waltke, and Paul and Gail Stevens, all of them with strings of degrees and scores of publications to their names. Initially, we felt like a couple of ignorant nobodies in the midst of these heroes of the faith. But our fears were soon put to rest. The wives all breathed a sigh of relief that, with us there, their husbands would no longer spend the evenings debating deep theological issues. And they all seemed to love our stories of faith at work and in God's amazing provision for our family. Though we now live far

137

apart from these precious men and women, we still count them as close friends, friends born out of deep heart fellowship (or as they would say, using the Greek, *koinonia*)!

All three of our girls spent that "Armerding year" with us. Laurie's health issues did not allow her to hold a regular job as a dental assistant, so she stayed home and became our one-and-only staff person with YWAM Associates International, our new ministry to the alumni of YWAM. She was instrumental in helping us begin reaching out to the alumni of YWAM worldwide through a little magazine we called *inTouch*. Julie spent the year at college studying special education, and Michelle was enrolled in college as well, taking an executive secretarial course.

During this time, Donna and I encountered an unfamiliar struggle—we fell into debt. We'd had a credit card for several years and had always managed to stay "paid up." If we knew we didn't have the money or didn't know where it was coming from, we didn't spend it. Living in Vancouver, we discovered that we could buy groceries using a credit card—a new experience for us. Rather quickly, we found it convenient to use our credit card in other ways, and the frequent flyer miles we earned would enable us to travel so much cheaper. After a few months of this, one day we woke up and realized we owed Visa close to $4,000, but we only had enough money to make the minimum payment. The interest rate was horrific, and we were horrified at ourselves. We took immediate steps to dig ourselves out of this pit. We confessed to God and to each other and then made a plan to be free from debt in four months. Our plan was simple: don't buy anything that isn't absolutely necessary. It wasn't easy, but by the grace of God we were free from our debt in just under four months. And we vowed we would never let that happen again.

After our first year in Vancouver, the shape of our family changed dramatically. In cultures that practice arranged marriages, typically the oldest daughter gets married first, then the next youngest, and so on down the line. But that's not how it happened in our family. God, it seemed, had a different plan.

From a young age, Michelle had felt that God had given her a special friendship with a young man named Mark West, whose family had joined the mission in Kona. He was the same Mark West who had helped in the renovation of our apartment, and he had since returned to Australia to finish high school and move on to university. Because Michelle was only fourteen years old when she declared her affection for Mark, the rest of us thought it was just puppy love. Time and distance would quickly dissolve whatever relationship she thought they had.

Convinced that Mark was "the one," Michelle prayed for him every day and wrote to him faithfully over the next three years until she graduated from high school. Throughout this time, she didn't date any other boys, though there were certainly a few bees buzzing around the hive. Then God told her it was time to go to a Discipleship Training School before she settled into her life's calling, whatever that might be. At the time, she was showing interest in and actually doing some modeling.

When Michelle asked the Lord where she should go for her DTS, she sensed him say, "Australia." The answer confused her at first; because she was convinced her desire to be near Mark—who by this time had a steady girlfriend in Australia—was preventing her from truly hearing God's voice. Finally, she came to Donna and me in tears and told us what was going on. We went to God for a confirmation, and it wasn't long before we were able to agree that Michelle had indeed heard from the Lord. He was calling her to the land Down Under. How Mark factored into that calling, we had no idea, because his plans appeared not to include Michelle.

In September of 1985, I flew over to Honolulu with Michelle on the first leg of her journey. After we went to see the movie *Back to the Future* together, I kissed her goodbye and put her on a 747 bound for Sydney. As the gigantic aircraft pushed back, I saw her face framed in a window—a face that reflected excitement, sadness, anticipation, and perhaps a tinge of fear at what lay ahead.

Mark's family were the only people we knew in Sydney, so we had asked his parents if they would meet Michelle at the airport and help her to get to the DTS base, which was in another city. Since Mark had a girlfriend, we assumed he would stay out of the picture. But as Michelle emerged from the Sydney airport bright and early the next morning, there was Mark, with his brother Jeremy, waiting to welcome her to their land. We didn't know it until later, but within a few days of that meeting, Mark's "steady" became history. When Mark had known Michelle back in Hawaii, she was barely a teenager. Now a young woman, she must have made quite an impression, because as soon as he saw her, he knew he loved her. It was as if they had never been apart.

The DTS rules regarding dating were strict, so Michelle only got to see Mark a couple of times—and then under watchful eyes. But she thoroughly enjoyed her five months Down Under, including an outreach that took her back and forth by bus across the entire width of Australia. En route, she helped pioneer a new missionary base in Perth, which continues to thrive to this day under the leadership of Peter and Shirley Brownhill. Peter was the young man to whom we gave our last ten dollars back in 1976 in our first school.

Upon her return to Kona, Michelle worked in an ice cream parlor and saved her money in the hope of returning to Australia. Knowing of Michelle's desire to return to the land Down Under, Tom and Diana Hallas, YWAM's Australia directors, asked if she would come and nanny for them for a few months.

It appeared that God was smiling on Michelle and Mark's relationship, and we all felt that he approved of her plans to return to Australia. Michelle's interest in modeling was also increasing. Though we had some doubts about that sort of a career direction in general, our trust in Michelle was solid. After six months of fulfilling her nanny duties, doing modeling (which was losing some of its charm), and seeing Mark more frequently, Michelle's visa expired and she had to leave the young man and the nation that she loved more and more each day.

When Michelle returned to Canada with us in early 1988, she enrolled in a computer course, with the aim of becoming an executive secretary. Mark was also in school, well on his way to becoming a mechanical engineer. Since it was summer in Australia, Mark was able to come and stay with us during our first Christmas back in Canada. Following Christmas, Donna and I left the three girls and Mark to care for the rented home in Vancouver in which we lived, while we returned to Kona to direct one more Crossroads DTS.

Laurie was still struggling with the chronic sicknesses that had plagued her for many years. So when a call came through for me in Hawaii in the middle of a class one morning, we feared the worst. I sprinted the one hundred yards to the phone, flip-flops flying in all directions. When I reached the phone, the back of my shirt wet with sweat, I gasped a breathless "Hello!" into the receiver. It was Mark. That didn't surprise me; I assumed the girls would have him call if there was bad news about Laurie. What did surprise me was that he didn't want to talk about Laurie. He wanted to talk about Michelle.

"G'day!" he drawled in his broad Australian accent. "May I marry Michelle?"

There's nothing like getting right to the point, I thought to myself. I was so relieved to find out Laurie was okay that I simply wheezed, "Of course." A second later, I realized the dirty rotten scoundrel had aced me. I had told myself for years that any guy who asked to marry one of my daughters would receive a thorough cross-examination. He would come out of it knowing I cared enough about my girls that I wouldn't give them away to just anybody! But in that moment, all of my cool questions went out the window.

And so it was that just before the following Christmas, the whole Jordan tribe found itself Down Under for an Australian wedding in the nation's capital, Canberra. After a beautiful ceremony officiated by Tom Hallas and a five-star reception put on by the leaders and staff at the YWAM base, it was one down and two to go. With Michelle successfully launched into married life, we could breathe a sigh of contentment and move on with life and ministry. Or could we?

Scarcely two weeks later, as Donna and I were sleeping off nasty doses of jet lag in Singapore, the raucous ringing of the bedside telephone awoke us at three o'clock in the morning. "Please, Lord, may it not be Laurie in the hospital again," was my silent prayer. After Michelle's wedding, young Pete had returned to Honolulu while Laurie had flown back to Vancouver, so we were thousands of miles and more than twenty-four agonizing hours of air travel away from her. I was not ready to board another airplane right then! But to my immediate relief, it was not Laurie on the phone, or anyone in Canada. But the origin of the call still caused some concern, because it was from the South Pacific island of Samoa, where Julie had flown off to visit a certain friend and his family. Little did I realize that, for the second time, I was about to be blindsided by a suitor for another of my daughters.

As I have already recounted, in 1982 the Island Breeze team joined the Kona base and brought with them a joy and a "whoop-it-up" vibrancy that we didn't even know we were missing. Housing on our base was in short supply, and it appeared as though the Island Breezers would have to live out in the community of Kona. This would have certain advantages, but it would also deprive us of their *joie de vivre* for much of each day. Around that time, some friends of ours who owned a small macadamia nut farm high up on the slopes of Mount Hualalai asked us to house-sit for them while they were on the US Mainland. We accepted their offer gladly, because it would allow us to enjoy the cooler temperatures in the evening. Seeing as our two-room apartment would be empty each night, we offered it to Island Breeze for the duration of the summer. Five of their girls moved in right away.

We didn't realize until years later that for the Polynesians, this simple act of hospitality bonded them to us, and we unwittingly became inducted into their family and culture. Before long, they began referring to Donna and me as "Mom" and "Dad." Our fridge became their fridge.[1] Food is an enormously important part of their culture, and many matters are sealed around a meal.

Even before Island Breeze arrived, Julie had fallen in love with Island culture. Some of her closest friends were Hawaiian. After graduating from high school, she joined Island Breeze in a service capacity. The Breezers were reaching out into the community and putting on godly entertainment for *luaus* (Hawaiian feasts) in local hotels. Julie handled costumes, helped the girls with their quick changes backstage, and served in many other ways.

In 1986, after spending several weeks on outreach in the Solomon Islands, God called Julie to Samoa to help staff a DTS and serve her good friends Ieru and Karen To'omua, who had a year-old baby. After more than a year in Samoa, familiarizing herself with the Island ways, Julie returned to Hawaii, right at the time that Donna and I were about to move back to Canada.

By this time the entire family knew two things: that Julie would only marry the one God wanted for her, and that he would have brown skin. But there was a problem. With no young man in her life, Julie was saddled with a tough decision: should she accompany her mom and dad back to Canada, as Laurie and Michelle were planning to do? Or should she stay in Hawaii? What chance would there be to meet an Islander in cold Canada?

Upon asking the Lord what to do, she felt—and we happily confirmed—that she was to return to Canada with us and enroll in a course on caring for children with special needs at a college in Vancouver. Barely after we had settled in Vancouver, we received a knock at our door. An outreach team from New Zealand, which was about to head home after ministry in British Columbia, had heard through the Coconut Wireless (that amazing means of Islander-to-Islander communication in the days before e-mail) that the Jordan family was in town. Could they

---

1. An Islander will only feel at home if, when he enters your house, he can immediately open the fridge to check it out—not necessarily to help himself, just to check it out!

crash on our living room floor? Of course they could. We enjoyed a terrific evening together.

One of the team leaders was Vaeluaga (Vae) Eli, a young man from Samoa. As he flew out of Vancouver a week later, heading toward a year-long commitment in the Cook Islands, he said to the Lord, "If I am to be married some day, let it be to a woman like Julie Jordan." At the time, he was thinking mostly in terms of a brown-skinned girl who had Julie's personality and character.

Over the next year as Vae led a small team of Cook Islanders around those far-flung dots of land on the South Pacific Ocean, God directed him to bring his team to Canada for several months in 1989. He wrote to Julie, asking her to coordinate things and plan an itinerary. Perhaps not coincidentally, God also started speaking to Vae about marriage. Vae made a list of the qualities he felt would be important to have in a wife. Then he compiled a list of all the girls he knew, carefully eliminating the ones who didn't fit. Eventually, he was left with just one name—Julie. Vae was filled with fear because he was convinced he had no chance with a *Palagi* ("white girl"). He sought the counsel of his leaders and others whose opinions he trusted. To his surprise, they all said, "Go for it!"

A letter in the mail expressing his heart and proposing a special relationship is not the way of an Islander. Such matters require a personal touch. But with six months before the team would arrive in Canada, Vae didn't know if he could wait. It so happened that David, a Samoan friend, was passing through the Cook Islands on his way to Vancouver. Vae seized the opportunity to compose a letter for David to hand-deliver to Julie. It merely suggested that the Lord had spoken to Vae about them having a relationship. Vae gave David strict instructions to observe Julie's reaction closely when she opened the letter. Thinking it was just a piece of correspondence about logistical matters for the upcoming outreach, when Julie received the letter, she opened it casually. But as she began to read it, her faced turned pale, and she ran for the safety of her bedroom.

That night, as Julie was in bed, she sobbed to the Lord, "I thought this was just a friendship for the purpose of planning and helping with the outreach. I respect him as a man of God, he's good-looking, has a great sense of humor, and has the same call on his life as I do, but I have no feelings for him." Finally, unable to sleep, Julie asked the Lord for a sign. "If you are in favor of this relationship, Lord, would you give me some feelings for Vae?" The next morning, she awoke with those feelings, together with a strong peace and excitement. She wrote to Vae and confirmed what he had been sensing from the Lord.

The summer and fall of 1989 were a major testing ground for Vae and Julie's fledgling relationship. Besides plain old misunderstandings between Vae and Julie, Vae, who is a deep thinker, also faced challenges in leading a team of Cook Islanders who had never been away from home.[2] It was overwhelming for Vae at times, and there were many painful silences. Sometimes the rest of us had little hope that anything would come of Julie and Vae's relationship.[3]

All of this was happening in the lead-up to Michelle and Mark's wedding. Laurie and Julie, who were bridesmaids, left for Australia just a few days before Vae's team disbanded and went back home. At that point, matters between Julie and Vae were at a standstill. As I drove Laurie and Julie to the Seattle airport, Julie lay in the backseat and sobbed all the way. When I returned to our home in Vancouver I was met by a dismal and

2. The two guys and two girls on the team had never been in an elevator, let alone experienced western culture. When they traveled by van around British Columbia, their eyes were spinning. They didn't know there was that much land all in one place! It takes only thirty minutes to drive all the way around their island. In later years, two of these four neophytes went on to become missionaries in India and Burma. Another became a nurse in New Zealand, and the fourth a pastor in Australia. From humble beginnings . . .

3. All through that challenging summer, I couldn't help thinking of Lysander's words from Shakespeare's *A Mid-Summer Night's Dream*: "The course of true love never did run smooth." If that were true, I thought that Vae and Julie must have been on the road to true love!

depressed team of Islanders. They were also crying because Julie was gone.

Before Vae returned to Samoa, he wrote a letter to Julie asking if she would come to Samoa for Christmas. Conventional wisdom said she shouldn't do that without some sort of commitment from Vae. But conventional wisdom is not always God's wisdom. In deep turmoil over this decision, Julie asked God what he thought, and she sensed him telling her to go.

Which brings us back to Donna and I lying jet-lagged in Singapore a few days after Christmas, with the phone jangling in our ears at three in the morning. It was Vae calling from Samoa. Had something happened to Julie? *She must be sick,* I thought. Wrong again. Vae explained that he had been trying to call me for a few days, but telephone service in the islands was poor. He had to travel two hours from his village to the nearest phone, and this was the only opportunity he had. I still hadn't caught on to why he had called, and so I got blindsided for the second time.

"I've called to ask if I can marry Julie," Vae said through the static-ridden phone connection. Looking over at Donna for confirmation, I gave a brilliant and insightful reply: "Sure. What took you so long?" I was desperate to think of something more intelligent to say, but nothing came to my foggy brain. After a short conversation with Julie to be sure she was okay with this surprising turn of events, I hung up. Then Donna and I prayed for the new couple and sought the sleep that so easily eludes those suffering from jet lag.

Only five short months after Michelle's wedding, Julie and Vae felt they were to plan for theirs. How would we ever be able to afford two weddings so close together? God had miraculously supplied a superb wedding for Michelle, but did we have the faith to believe the Lord would do it again so soon? Friends and family had given so generously to make Michelle's wedding a success. Would another one so soon afterward put a strain on those cherished relationships? With our bank account happily reduced to zero, these questions and more assailed us.

Knowing that we must ask our Father who loves us and cares for us and knows our needs, we prayed, "Lord, you see our hearts. You know if Julie and Vae are ready to be married. You also understand what this is going to cost. Should we go ahead with it?" This sort of simple and direct question is not too difficult for any loving father to answer. A deep peace settled over us. All the fears and doubts that we might have had about Julie and Vae's often-stormy relationship were swept away.

Since Julie had spent most of her formative years in Hawaii, many of our friends still lived there, and it would be the easiest place for Vae's family to reach, we asked the Kona base leaders if they would be willing to host the wedding reception. They responded with open arms in true "aloha" style. The wedding ceremony was set in the lush tropical gardens of a nearby hotel on a manicured lawn that swept down to the ocean. Surrounded by swaying palms, brilliant hibiscus bushes, fragrant plumeria trees, and many witnesses, Vae and Julie were married. The party that followed was pure Island delight, with the swaying rhythms of the Island Breeze band and a fabulous feast around the fountain of the Plaza of Nations, put on by the staff of the University of the Nations. Once again, we had had a huge wedding and walked away without any debt. How did we manage it? We didn't. Our Father in heaven did it through the kindness and generosity of his people.

— *Chapter 14* —

The House of Peace

Our year in the lap of luxury in the Armerdings' home was followed by four years of nomadic sojourning in an assortment of rented, borrowed, and squatted-in digs. With Michelle and Julie now married off, we established ourselves in a modest apartment in Richmond. This suburb of Vancouver was rapidly becoming an Asian center because of the many immigrants pouring in from Hong Kong (much to my delight, since choices for good Chinese food multiplied!). Together with Laurie, our faithful assistant-in-everything, we lived in the midst of what had become the YWAM Associates International office, a shoe-box-sized bedroom in our simple three-room flat. Not only was this our base of operations; it also served as a crash pad for other sojourners.

In early 1992 Wayne and Nancy-Jane Johnson, with their two young daughters, Meghan and Andrea, came to join us for the year. They were inspirational, visionary, and servant-hearted during the course of the major transitional events that soon followed. Wayne, having been a salesman before joining YWAM, took on the job of finding and buying a brand-new, rock-bottom-priced minivan that we needed for the ministry. Nancy-Jane was a prayer warrior and a woman of God. She and Wayne were a tremendous support to us in those foundational days as we pioneered renewal camps (one-week "vacations with a purpose" for alumni) and continued growing the alumni magazine *inTouch*, whose circulation was now into the thousands—and also costing thousands!

During this time, Donna and I had "adopted" Mark and Rebekah Lee, a newly married couple from Singapore. Mark, a businessman, and Rebekah, a preschool teacher working at a bank, became our close friends. They were a constant blessing to the ministry and to us, and still are. Hardly a week went by without them taking us out for dinner (salt-and-pepper crab was my favorite) or coming to our place to enjoy an evening together.

All Chinese women are supposed to be able to cook, but Rebekah was so focused on her job that she had little time or inclination for the kitchen. She could barely boil an egg, and I could only imagine what her mother thought about that. (Fortunately, Mark was an accomplished chef.) I'm a bit of a leg-puller, and Rebekah is an "easy tease," though she gives as good as she gets. One time Rebekah's mom and aunt visited from Singapore, and we were duly invited to meet them for dinner at a Chinese restaurant. We were the last to arrive, and upon being introduced to the two women, I immediately complimented Rebekah's mother on her wonderful daughter and her daughter's gifted ways in the kitchen. Everybody laughed—except Rebekah, who fixed me with her famous "stink eye." Today, Rebekah has an important position in a well-known multinational company.

Julie and her husband, Vae, were also frequent visitors. They had started a ministry called Pacific Waves, discipling Pacific Islanders who reached out to the aboriginal people of Canada's First Nations. It wasn't long before our apartment was bursting at the seams, especially when Julie brought forth her first child, Leilani ("heavenly flower"). We needed more space, but how would we get it? Richmond's real estate market was skyrocketing because of the people and money fleeing Hong Kong in response to the impending handover of that great city-state back to China after ninety-nine years of British rule. It was during those exciting and unsettling times that the improbable notion of buying a house for the ministry came up. Was this the Lord speaking?

We had always dreamed of having a place where weary missionaries and other ministers of the gospel could find peace and quiet for a few days, a place where they would be renewed and refreshed. Could this be the beginning of that dream's fulfillment? One thing was certain: if we were to buy a house, it would have to be a miracle. We had no funds with which to make such a purchase. Just to run out of fax paper, not to mention paying the rent and buying food, was a major financial crisis during that time. But I knew that God seemed to enjoy dropping his kids in the deep end and watching them flounder (in faith, of course!) before gently guiding them toward safer waters where they could watch his vision unfold. So we prepared ourselves for a new leap of faith.

By this time, we knew what it meant to live hand to mouth—or, to put it in more spiritual terms, we knew how to live by faith. But we never went hungry. Like George Müller's orphans who were seated at their tables with no food in sight when the clip-clop of horse's hooves announced the arrival of the baker with miracle bread, so it was with us regarding some of the tools we needed to carry on the ministry. Publishing *inTouch* three times a year and mailing it all over the world was both a joy and a challenge. Printing and postage costs alone were already up to US$5,000 per edition.[1] Faith in God's ability to provide all of

1. After seventeen years and fifty editions, *inTouch* was eventually mailed to more than 30,000 readers in 160 countries. The US$5,000 cost grew to $12,000, three times a year. And God supplied each time, though on more than one occasion I walked into the print shop with artwork for the next *inTouch* in one hand and the final payment for the previous edition clutched in the other. Thank you, Glenn Rowley, of Glenmore Printing in Richmond, BC!

our needs grows over time, just as regular exercise makes muscles bigger and stronger.[2] We certainly had our share of regular faith workouts!

Around this time, Laurie was out for a walk when she noticed a house for sale. She sensed a twinge of the Spirit and came home and told us about it. After Donna and I drove by, we dismissed it as being too big (it looked like two houses connected at right angles on a corner lot) and therefore too expensive for what we imagined our budget to be. But Laurie began praying for some way that we might purchase that house. As weeks went by, the house failed to sell, and the sign was taken down. But Laurie did not give up praying.

Then one day, as Laurie was walking to the store, she saw someone hammering a "For Sale" sign into the ground outside what she had now come to think of as "her" house. It was back on the market. This time all three of us went and looked through the house, and we saw its tremendous potential as a house of hospitality. Thus, the House of Peace vision was conceived, and we began to seek the Lord about buying it. We sensed he was encouraging us to take the plunge, but there was just one problem: we didn't even have enough to make the $1,000 good faith deposit, never mind buying the house outright. Were we dreaming, or was God really speaking this vision into reality? The possible purchase of this house was peanuts compared to buying the hotel property back in Kona. Maybe, just maybe, God had used the Kona exercise to develop our faith muscles for such a time as this.

One day, Pastor Bob Birch, a man of God in his eighties who had the nation of Canada etched across his heart, paid us a visit. As we chatted over a cup of tea, he asked about the ministry. We recounted some key events from the past four years and then, quite naturally, brought up our vision for the House of Peace. When we were finished, Pastor Bob stunned us by quietly remarking, "We're on holy ground." Then he departed, leaving us blessed by

2. See 2 Thessalonians 1:3.

his visit but also a bit puzzled by his cryptic remark. We didn't stay puzzled for long.

Early the next morning, the buzzer summoned me downstairs to the front door of our apartment building. There, to my great surprise, stood Pastor Bob. He was shivering with cold, only partially sheltered from the bitter and blustery winter rain that soaked his raincoat. As soon as I opened the door, he thrust an envelope into my hand and said, "God bless you!" Declining my invitation to come in and dry off, that very special, elderly man of prayer got back into his car to battle his way through Vancouver's heavy morning rush hour traffic for the sixty-minute drive home.

I carried the envelope upstairs to Donna and Laurie, wondering what was inside. When I ripped it open, all three of us jumped for joy. It was a check for $1,000! We all knew what this meant: the House of Peace was on its way! We had moved from vision to reality.

Later, we learned that Pastor Bob had been up since 2:00 AM, praying for our ministry and the House of Peace. He felt the Lord leading him and his dear wife, Margaret, to make a contribution. Little did we or the Birches realize that their first donation, a good-sized "snowball," would create just enough momentum to precipitate an avalanche of generosity that would eventually come crashing down upon us from all over the world.

We submitted the vision to our board of directors, who encouraged us to go ahead. We made what we felt was a fair offer on the house—an amount we sensed the Lord had given. It was accepted, and we handed over the precious and highly significant $1,000 deposit. We were acutely aware that we had a long road of faith ahead of us before we could take possession, but we were on the way!

As the months rolled on and summer arrived, a few small donations came in. These enabled us to obtain a mortgage, which was signed for while we were leading an alumni renewal camp in California. Final details of the purchase were accomplished through a flurry of telephone calls and faxes between Fred Warkentin, our real estate agent and a former YWAMer, and us.

Now came the real test: the down payment of $10,000. In the *natural*, we couldn't see any way that this could happen, let alone how we could ever make the huge closing payment when we were to take possession of the house later in the year. But we had a *supernatural* God whose word to us was to "move ahead." We had done the possible, and we knew enough by then to leave the impossible up to God.

Two dear friends were at that renewal camp in California— Dan Sneed (one of our board members) and Glenn Sheppard. Both had been pastors in the traditional sense but had gone on to become itinerant ministers. Together with their wives, Bev and Jackie, they had been students in a Discipleship Training School that Donna and I had led a few years earlier. Upon hearing of our situation, they put their heads together in prayer and felt God leading them to take an offering right then and there for the House of Peace. Together with what we had already saved, those at the camp gave enough for us to meet the $10,000 deposit.

But Dan and Glenn weren't finished. They wrote a letter to our entire *inTouch* mailing list, which was being mailed to almost ten thousand people at that time. They laid out our vision for the House of Peace as well as our needs, the main one being the "take possession" payment, which was due in October. (It was already June.) We were so thankful for their help. But after we printed the letter, there was just one problem—it was going to cost us $5,000 for postage! Like typical visionaries, Dan and Glenn encouraged us to work through such "minor" details in faith. Even though we didn't have the money, we planned to manually prepare the mailing at a renewal camp to be held in August.

Knowing that God wouldn't bring us this far only to abandon us, we asked him for wisdom regarding how to pay for the postage. As we were getting ready to head off for camp, John DeVries, faithful donor of our fax machine and even some of the endless rolls of the paper it consumed, was on his way into Vancouver when he called us on his cell phone. (John and Sandra and their kids had been to a couple of our camps in Idaho, and their children were going into YWAM schools.) "Do you have any needs right now?" John asked. Did we? Upon hearing about the cost of the mailing, he calmly replied, "I'll cover that."

And so off we went to the August camp on a Native American reservation in Washington State. It was on the most northwesterly point of the original forty-eight states, just across the Strait of Juan de Fuca from Victoria, BC. Now that we had the $5000 for postage, our plan was to enlist some volunteers and use our afternoons at camp to prepare the ten thousand letters for mailing—inserting, sealing, and sticking stamps and address labels on each envelope.

When we finished "licking and sticking," we dropped the letters off at the local post office, from which they would be sent all over the world. Now all we could do was wait—and wonder. What would the response be? Such letters are commonplace in the West, but how would this sort of appeal be received in Bangladesh, Bahrain, or Budapest? We knew the letter would need a special anointing.

Soon, responses started coming in from all over the planet. Some said they couldn't help us financially but that they would join with us in prayer. Others sent a couple dollars or whatever they could manage. Many other gifts, both small and large, poured in. Laurie kept track of them all in a memory book. All told, we received responses from people in sixty-two nations. When the day came for us to take possession of the house, we had just enough money to satisfy the conditions of the mortgage. It was a joyful day as many of our friends rallied around to help with the heavy work of moving into the new House of Peace. Among those friends were Gary and Diana Chang from Hawaii, longtime friend Dorothy Wong, Mark and Rebekah Lee (of course), and Wayne and Nancy Johnson, our other staff members.

We lived in that house for seven wonderful years. During that time, we hosted hundreds of friends old and new, held seminars, and celebrated anything and everything worth celebrating. Our staff ebbed and flowed (like any missions base), and we welcomed into our team not only the Johnson family but also Patrick and Inneke Elaschuk (right off their honeymoon), Lilo Ainuu, Dan and Diane Dyck, wonderful Wanda Pickett, Wrenetta (Willms) Sinclair, May Dinardo, Barbara Pybus, and many others who pitched in from day to day. Malcolm and Rosalie Heath joined us from New Zealand. Malcolm was a bit of a genius and a jack of all trades. He could handle heavy equipment like bulldozers, and he knew anything worth knowing about computers and how they function. He was also pretty good at everything else in between. Rosalie—or "Roses," as our young grandson Tavita called her— was Mrs. Hospitality and took care of much of the running of the house.

We developed our own way of publishing and distributing *inTouch*. This included writing, editing, gathering photos, designing, printing, folding, inserting, gluing, and stamping.[3] When all of the components were ready, we would gather thirty to forty friends and blitz the job. We called these volunteer events "Lick 'em and Stick 'em" parties. Yes, parties. A wider family team was surely being established. To this day, we still hear from people saying, "I wish we still had those times together." We worked hard, prayed for every piece of paper that passed through our hands, ate well, and had a lot fun.[4]

---

3. Yes, we stuck postage stamps on each and every envelope until the circulation passed ten thousand, when I finally bowed to the inevitable and we changed to bulk mailing.

4. While I was out running an errand during one of our Lick 'em and Stick 'em parties, Rebekah Lee rounded everyone up, formed a union, and took a strike vote demanding higher wages, more breaks, and better food. They even made up placards. When I returned, they were picketing and marching around outside the House of Peace. Even Laurie's little puppy, DJ, carried a sign reading "More Treats." I laughed so hard I almost drove into the ditch.

— Chapter 15 —

Life in Paradise

Then one day we sensed the Lord saying, "It's time to move 'up the valley' and out of the city." Our initial response was, "Where, Lord? And why?" I felt much the same as I did when Donna had begun to feel God calling us away from Kona. After seven years in the House of Peace, why on earth would God ask us to move? We were well established in a local church, we had made many friends, and the ministry—though always challenging in one area or another—was going well. God was providing mortgage payments each month, *inTouch* financially squeaked out three times a year, and all of our other expenses were somehow covered.[1] Admittedly, there were times when we waited with bated breath for another miracle of provision, but we were content, so what was God up to? Why mess with a good thing?

As we thought about it more, we realized that Richmond was growing. What had been a relatively quiet neighborhood was

---

1. In YWAM, no one gets paid. Each person, each family, is responsible before God to "pray in" their support.

now bustling with all the usual city sights and sounds—traffic and sirens night and day on a street that never used to see such things. It was no longer the peaceful environment we craved.

So in January 1999, we dutifully called our good friend Fred Warkentin, who had helped us buy the House of Peace seven years previously, and asked him to start the selling process. To our amazement, in a very short time we had three offers with each potential buyer outbidding the previous one. We settled on a price that was $10,000 more than what we were asking (in a market that had fluctuated, mostly down, during our seven-year stay). The only catch was that we had to vacate the house by the end of March. It was now mid-February. We had only six weeks, and nowhere to go. The family that bought the house were Zoro-astrians who came to Canada originally from India, though their ethnicity was Persian. Some traditions say that the Wise Men who visited Jesus were Zoroastrians. In any case, one of the women in this large family who initially came to see the house clutched Donna's arm and said, "God's presence is here!" She insisted to her husband that they buy this house—and they did.

As the date of our imminent departure drew near, Donna, who had a headache, decided to stay home from church one Sunday and seek the Lord. "Father, so much is happening," she prayed. "Our home, your house, has sold, and we have no place to go. We've looked up and down the valley, and I know the places we saw aren't what you want us to have." Back came the Father's reply: "My daughter, rest in me; you have been obedient in put-ting the house up for sale, now rest." Then her heavenly Father went on to tell her that "the Deroche property" was to be our destination.

The Deroche property was a forty-acre piece of land located seventy miles east of Vancouver in a tiny unincorporated hamlet named Deroche. The land lay on the side of a mountain overlook-ing the Fraser Valley. It was covered in majestic, ancient fir trees, had a river running through it, and, most importantly, boasted a large, rustic, old house. The property was being used mostly for weekend retreats. We had even held a few of our board meetings in this little piece of earthly heaven. It was one of the most beautiful corners of God's planet.

The property had been placed in a trust by Donna's cousin Bill McAllister and his wife, Jean. After moving to Vancouver, we had quickly latched onto Bill and Jean as friends, and Bill became our first board member. Over the years, we relied heavily on his business expertise, wisdom, and counsel. He was also a frequent visitor to the House of Peace.

As soon as Donna told Laurie and I what she had heard, we scrambled around trying to find Bill and Jean's phone number in Arizona, where they were enjoying an extended winter stay. When we finally got it, we phoned and told them what we felt the Lord had said. There was a long silence on the other end of the line, and then Bill said, "Unfortunately, just last week we rented it to a church, which plans to use it as a retreat center for the next year."

We were devastated. We had missed the boat! We didn't hear God right about selling the House of Peace, and now we were set up to look like fools. Disappointed, embarrassed, chagrined, despairing, we didn't know which way to turn. We figured we had no choice but to call off the sale. But legally, could we?

Two days later, we were still waiting upon the Lord, too afraid to tell anyone of our predicament, when the phone rang. It was Bill calling from Arizona. "You'll never believe what happened," he said, with excitement in his voice. "The church that planned to rent the Deroche house backed out of the contract! So if you still want it, it's yours."

Let me tell you, there was a lot of whooping and hollering that day as we celebrated God's faithfulness. We *had* heard from God after all!

For the next six years, we lived in one of the most beautiful spots on earth. Deer, black bears, coyotes, and foxes were our frequent visitors. And then there were the birds. I counted more than thirty species, from huge herons, owls, and bald and golden eagles down to the smallest birds on earth, the swooping, clicking, hovering, and ever-thirsty hummingbirds. As a lover of birds, it was a paradise for me.

And a river also ran through it. Well, it was more of a creek that pretty much dried up during the summer. River or creek, that's where we got our water, gravity-fed through a plastic pipe that ran underground to the picturesque old house that became our home, office, and hang-out for friends and family. Heavy winter rains—for which the west coast is known—brought many challenges to our water supply. The worst was when gravel and rocks blocked the intake pipe. This required someone to head up the mountain; slip and slide on the banks of the flooding creek; negotiate treacherous, moss-covered logs; and finally wade into the rushing, icy waters and grope around in the murk to free up the intake. Doing it in the daytime was difficult enough. Darkness brought on a whole new set of challenges—and fears. A few of our trusty staff made most of these brave forays, although I also went on a few hazardous missions. At such times, it felt like we were pioneers of old.

It wasn't long before Deroche grew into a bustling little community. Laurie, Malcolm and Rosalie Heath, Dan and Diane Dyck, Dwight and Bobbi Greiner, Dawn Michelle Newsham, Dora Klassen, Connie Schubert, Byron Hunt, Janet Chan, and others labored with us. Together we carried on all of the ministries we had been doing in Richmond and more. Both Donna and I traveled frequently in ministry, but we had such good people on our team that being away was never a concern.

Julie and Vae and their team lived nearby in the city of Abbotsford, on the Canada/US border. They were constant visitors, and their family (as well as their team) kept multiplying. By then they had four children, Leilani, Manu, Tavita, and Hannah. Their ministry focus among the First Nations peoples of Canada was leading them farther and farther east to the wide-open prairies beyond the Rocky Mountains, all the way into the wheat fields of Saskatchewan and beyond. Doors in that area were being flung open to their friendship ministry on the First Nations reservations. They already had a few Native Canadians on their team. But it was a long two- or three-day drive to reach those open doors. When the lease on their rental housing in Abbotsford ended, the Lord directed them to move the whole team to a small city in Alberta with the intriguing name of Medicine Hat.

Meanwhile, life in paradise was turning tough. Malcolm and Rosalie had returned to their home in New Zealand for health reasons.[2] Meanwhile, God was calling the rest of our staff away to other areas of ministry, and it looked like Donna, Laurie, and I would be on our own. After six years of being surrounded by the manifold beauties of God's creation and having a wonderful staff family, the Lord began preparing us to move once again.

As the winter of 2004/2005 was approaching, it appeared that we would have to face it alone. But with Donna and I traveling so much, there was no way we could leave Laurie by herself. Vae and Julie were now established in Medicine Hat, and we began to wonder if the Lord was also pointing us in that direction. Would it be wrong to ask God about moving closer to them? Would we be able to hear the Lord clearly? We needed some answers, so a visit to this strange-sounding place was next on our agenda. With little prospect of being able to build some sort of a new House of Peace (or even a few "Cabins of Peace"), we were feeling the nudge of God again. We wanted a clear word from the Lord if we

---

2. Malcolm had a pancreatic attack and spent almost a year in hospital, six weeks of which he was in the intensive care unit, where he was labeled the "sickest man in Vancouver." Twice when we visited him, we came upon this form of a man, propped up, glassy eyed, with a vacant stare and what seemed like dozens of tubes going in and out of various parts of him. He was surrounded by more monitors than you'll find in a TV store, a nurse on constant duty, and a doctor hovering nearby. Sometimes as we prayed for Malcolm, we were low in faith, convinced we would never see him again. To make matters worse, while Malcolm was enduring his trial, Rosalie required a serious operation. Thankfully, both of them recovered. God was good to us all. Malcolm lived for nine more productive years before "going home."

were to move. We would also need to give fair warning to Bill and Jean, our landlords.

In late November, Donna and I made the trek to "The Hat," as locals call Medicine Hat, a city about as different from Deroche as the arid Sahara Desert is to a lush and beautiful tropical island. Miles and miles of flat prairie surround this city of about sixty thousand souls. It's hot in the summer and cold in the winter, but there's a year-round warmth from its people. Immediately upon arrival, we were struck by the spirit of friendliness and hospitality that characterized the region.

While visiting with Vae and Julie and their kids, one morning we had breakfast with Wes and Janice Reinheller, community leaders with a long-established construction business. They quickly made us feel welcome and invited us to live and minister in their city. We drove away from The Hat with singing hearts. Could this be our new home? We had sought the counsel of others we respected, and by the time we returned to Deroche, we had received almost a dozen confirmations that this move was God's plan for us.

Even so, we sought one more confirmation. Imiel Abadir is an Egyptian-Canadian man of God whom we had come to know. He hears very clearly from the Lord, and we wanted to know what he might discern regarding our possible shift. On our way to the Vancouver airport, from which we would fly to spend Christmas in Australia with Michelle and her family, followed by a Renewal Camp near Sydney, we stopped at Imiel's home and asked him to seek the Lord about our move—of which he knew nothing up to that point. In his unique style of prayer, he rocked back and forth in his chair, closed eyes pointed heavenward, and waited for a word from the Lord. Then it came: "You are to move to Medicine Hat, and rivers (of ministry) will come together and flow from that place." There was more, but it all affirmed what God had been saying to us.

A couple hours later, as we stepped onto to the Sydney-bound airplane, we were confident that God had spoken and that we were to make the move to Medicine Hat. When we got to Australia, we contacted Bill and Jean and informed them of our decision to leave by mid-June.

After a wonderful Christmas with Mark and Michelle and their kids, we directed a renewal camp along with Peter and Beverley West (Michelle's in-laws) near Sydney. Laurie, who accompanied us, headed up the camp children's program. Next, we hopped over to New Zealand for another week-long camp. From New Zealand, Donna flew to Kona to teach in a DTS, and I returned home to a deserted, lonely, snowy house with blocked and frozen water pipes in Deroche. (Laurie would follow a few days later.) There was no way I could get through the deep, wet snow up at the creek to clear the gravel and debris from the water pipe. Besides, I was starting to feel very tired, and even walking up stairs left me breathless. I knew something was wrong with me, but I continued to soldier on, not bothering to tell anyone. (My family, when they heard what followed, accused me, rather unkindly I thought, of being independent!)

Thankfully, there was some drinking water in the house, but to flush the toilet I had to break the ice on the fishpond outside and then haul water inside by the bucketful. I felt like a pioneer of old, hauling water and splitting wood for the stove that heated the house. I might even have felt a tad sorry for myself. Soon, however, Laurie returned home from Australia, the ice and snow melted, and we had running water again. I still felt tired and breathless most of the time, but stubborn as always, I decided to fulfill a commitment to perform a wedding in Hawaii—over Laurie's objections. The plan was to meet Donna in Maui and then fly back with her to San Francisco, where she would stay to teach in another DTS while I returned home. My entire trip would last just three days.

On the way back, it was all I could do to drag myself through the airports. Donna was quite concerned about me, and she made me promise to get myself checked when I returned home. As soon as I landed in Vancouver, I called Laurie, who insisted that I not drive home alone. But her stubborn dad refused. I asked her to meet me at our local hospital, which was still more than an hour's drive from the airport. Thankfully, God overlooked my foolishness. When I got to the emergency room, Laurie was waiting for me, looking very concerned.

Upon checking my vital signs, the doctor told me I had *bradycardia*—a very slow heart rate. It was down as low as twenty beats per minute (sixty is the norm). No wonder I was breathless and tired! They rushed me off in an ambulance to the intensive care unit at another hospital, where I was fitted with a temporary external pacemaker. It got my heart going at the proper speed, and soon I was feeling much better. As I looked around the ICU at the people who were really sick, some even dying, I felt like a sham.

After a couple of days, they inserted a compact German pacemaker, less than half the size of an iPod, under the skin just below my left shoulder. This little miracle ticker has a battery that's supposed to last several years! As I adjusted to life with my new implanted friend, we realized that the timing of our upcoming move to Medicine Hat had to be of the Lord, because we could not have lived through another harsh and isolated Deroche winter.

And so it was to be "Eastward ho!" once more, though we didn't know what all this would entail. But God had more miracles up his sleeve.

Chapter 16

Miracles on the Way to The Hat

We didn't make the journey east through the mountains over bumpy roads in rickety covered wagons like the early pioneers when they headed west. We traveled on broad, scenic highways inside two comfy cars. We knew little of what God had in store for us in The Hat, but even as we set out toward our new home, God continued to confirm that we were on the right track.

The journey took four days. Donna traveled with Laurie to keep her company. I followed in our car accompanied by two other family members: Patches, Laurie's little Maltese Shih Tzu dog; and Joey, my cheerful yellow canary.[1] I kept in touch with Laurie and Donna via walkie-talkie.

---

1. Joey was named after JoEllyn Wright, and he sang along beautifully with her worship album, aptly named *The Journey*. Producing JoEllyn's album was one of the greatest satisfactions in my life. It all began when Donna and I heard JoEllyn in worship and were touched so deeply that I wanted to record her songs. Thanks to the leaders at the YWAM base in Chico, California, who made their recording facilities available, we were able to do just that.

Crossing the border from British Columbia into Alberta, we were greeted with torrential rain that lasted twenty-four hours. That night, we enjoyed the hospitality of Dawn Michelle Newsham, a former YWAM Associates staffer who was now managing a retreat center near Calgary. As we slept, the river that ran through the retreat center's property rose rapidly and washed away a bridge. When we continued our journey the next day, the rain was only just starting to let up. Back on the Trans-Canada Highway, we discovered that the four lanes behind us were now blocked for miles because of flooding. We had just made it through the night before!

Once we were past the beautiful city of Calgary nestled against the mighty Rocky Mountains, the skies finally cleared and we had a gorgeous, sunny Alberta day. Yet we heard on the radio that Medicine Hat—still three hours ahead of us—had just experienced an enormous thunderstorm with bucketing rain and hail as big as baseballs. When we drove into the city, we could see the damage that the freak storm had wrought—dented cars and roofs and the telltale signs of recent flash floods. We realized that not only had we been spared from long delays due to a flooded highway behind us, but the timing of our trip also protected us from the hailstorm just a few hours ahead. If we had left a day earlier or a day later, we would have had a different tale to tell. We felt terrible for those who suffered through the flooding and the smashing hailstorm, but we were also encouraged that God had shielded us from it all. This wasn't the first time during our move that we had experienced God's miraculous provision.

A few months earlier, after we had decided to leave beautiful British Columbia, we had to start thinking and praying about where we would live and have our ministry office once we transplanted to Medicine Hat. Would we rent or buy? At the time, our worldly possessions amounted to a pretty reliable four-year-old car and some comfortable but well-worn furniture, which we gave to Vae and Julie. Our prospects for buying our own accommodations seemed remote at best. The ministry, however, still had the proceeds from the sale of the Richmond House of Peace, which we had invested in some term deposits. This money—close to $200,000—had been waiting to be used to build a new House of Peace at Deroche. With those plans never having come to pass, the money was still available for a new ministry building.

Following my medical interlude when I was fitted with a pacemaker, Donna and I paid another visit to The Hat to check out possible housing. Our financial circumstances had not changed, but we sensed the Lord releasing us to purchase a house or a condo. The latter would have distinct advantages, allowing us to simply lock the door and walk away on our numerous ministry trips without worrying about who would cut the grass or who would do all the other chores that go along with home ownership. It was all a bit scary, because we really didn't want to own another property. We'd already been there, done that, in another life before missions.

Then one miserable, rainy day—a rarity in The Hat—Wes Reinheller, whose company built quality condominiums all over Canada, took us to see one of his creations, which was still partially under construction. Rather than leading us to a modest unit that we had been considering, one we felt we could possibly afford, he marched us straight up to one of the best apartments. It had an expansive view of the mighty South Saskatchewan River, which flowed right beneath the windows. The unit had only been framed so far. As the rain dripped all around us, Wes, with great conviction and enthusiasm, said, "I believe this is to be yours." When he proceeded to drop the price, we were tempted to just say, "We'll take it!" But though we sensed the Lord encouraging us, we needed to do a little bean counting—and praying—first. We had to make sure we could cover a mortgage if, and it was a big if, some bank would risk giving a mortgage to a missionary couple with no visible means of support.

Upon returning to Deroche, we started calculating a monthly payment we might be able to manage. I also contacted a pastor's wife I knew who arranged mortgages for a bank in Medicine Hat.

Back and forth we communicated until, to our amazement, she was able to work out a payment schedule that both the bank and Donna and I could live with. Feeling God's pleasure with the arrangement, we put a deposit on the condo. With the money from the old Richmond House of Peace, we also purchased another smaller condo unit for the YWAM Associates office. It was just down the hall from our unit, and there was enough to pay for it in cash, so there would be no mortgage on it at all. Laurie would live in it, run our office, and take care of the monthly maintenance fee with the support she received as a missionary.[2]

As the weeks rolled by, we knew we had to come up with a significant down payment to close the deal on our new condo home. Meanwhile, Donna continued her traveling ministry, teaching in various discipleship schools. In one Chinese school in Los Angeles, Donna was asked about our living conditions. She felt released to share about our upcoming move. Afterward, the school leader gave the students an opportunity to donate toward the purchase of our condominium. One couple came to Donna and said the Lord had told them to give $10,000! Even more poured in. Elsewhere, a Japanese friend heard about our impending move and e-mailed to say he had a bank account in the US that he had forgotten about and felt led to give us whatever was in it. It turned out to be several thousand dollars!

One day we received a phone call from a woman we knew from the church we had attended in Vancouver. She said, "As I was praying the other day, I heard the Lord say to me, 'Sell off your shares.' I said, 'Okay, Lord, but what shall I do with the money?' Right then it was like a picture of you two appeared before my eyes." We didn't ask her how much she was talking about, but we assumed it could be a couple thousand dollars, and we were suitably grateful. We seemed to be on a roll!

Then, while we were in California leading a Renewal Camp just days before our move, we received a phone call from this

2. This condo will eventually be sold and the proceeds will go toward the building of a new House of Peace in Medicine Hat.

woman, telling us she had finally freed up the money and was prepared to transfer it to us. How would we like to receive it? We told her that a wire transfer would be best, but she pressed further. "Don't you want to know how much it is?"

"Well . . . yes," I replied hesitantly.

"Two hundred and forty-six thousand dollars!" was her incredible rejoinder. Whew! This certainly put my new pacemaker to the test! Figures flashed through my mind as I tried to calculate what this meant. Added to what we had already been given, I realized we had enough to walk straight into the condominium mortgage-free. Lord, how could this be? We were overcome with gratefulness to God and to everyone else who had made this miracle possible. In the midst of our celebration, we couldn't help thinking back to the time when we didn't even have thirty-five cents to do laundry. Now we found ourselves in the position of owning a home with no mortgage, and having enough left over to buy some new furniture!

After forty-three years of missionary service in China, my father had left his four children with a tremendous spiritual inheritance, but he did not leave us much in the way of a financial windfall. Not that we expected anything. It was never a source of contention in our family. So when I did receive an inheritance check in the mail following Dad's death, I was a surprised—until I opened it and saw that it was for $64! I had a good laugh. It was $64 more than I expected! My mother's inheritance was mostly spiritual too, though she had somehow enabled me to go to a very good private school as a teenager.

Many years after my parents passed on to their reward, I received another unexpected inheritance. It was like a message from heaven from my mother and father—and the countless other missionaries who had sowed their lives into the soil of China—who never lived to see the current harvest of souls in that nation.

During the 1990s, Donna and I were able to spend more than one vacation in Florida. Marney, Donna's oldest sister, and her husband, John, allowed us to stay in their time-share apartment on the beach at Cape Canaveral, where spacecraft launches occur. Nearby Port Canaveral also happens to be the home port of Disney cruise ships. One evening at sunset, we were walking around the harbor when the enormous *Disney Magic* cast off its lines and headed out to sea. Hundreds of families lined the railings and waved excitedly as they left on their holiday adventure. The ship's horn bellowed out the tune of "When You Wish upon a Star." At that idyllic moment, I don't know if it was a wish or a prayer that went through my mind, but I found myself thinking, *Wouldn't it be wonderful if our whole family could do this?* Then I put the thought away as too fantastic.

A couple of years later, I was glancing through the *Vancouver Sun* newspaper when a tiny headline over a one-paragraph news item caught my eye: "Japanese Government Makes Reparations with British Prisoners of War in Asia." I read on with increasing excitement as the details were spelled out. The Japanese government would give £10,000 (about US$17,000 at the time) to any British citizen who had been a POW in Asia during the war. I couldn't believe it—I fit the bill! I wasted no time in applying, and within two months the money was in my bank account. My brother and sister, who were skeptical at first, also cashed in on the windfall.

I had no doubt about how my money was to be spent: a Disney cruise and a few days at Disneyworld in Florida for our family. Because Julie and Michelle were both in the childbearing mode of their lives, we had to wait two years for the big event. Finally, I called our travel agent and said, "Book us the best Disney package seventeen thousand dollars can buy!" It's not often you can say something like that.

So it happened that in early December 2003, fifteen of us set out on a once-in-a-lifetime adventure. Donna and I had saved up our frequent flyer miles for several years and were able to fly Michelle and her family all the way from Australia as well as nine more of our family from Canada.[3] It was a memorable time, and

3. Sadly, Pete was not well enough to travel at the time.

to this day we are thankful to God—and my mom and dad—for such a surprising and unexpected inheritance. I am convinced that God directed my eyes to that squib in the newspaper, which I could have easily missed.

All of these memories of God's miraculous provision came flooding back as we prepared to begin another new chapter in our lives. Our ministry didn't change when we moved to The Hat; it was simply transplanted to a new location, complete with new friends added to our ever-expanding circle of relationships. From day one in The Hat, we felt nothing but welcome as well as a sense of anticipation about what God would do in this next season of our lives.

— *Chapter 17* —

The Waiting Father

For the first forty-one years of my life, I had made a private deal with God that went something like this: I will be a faithful churchgoer, but the last thing I will do is be a missionary. By now, you should have a pretty clear idea of what that got me—a life sentence! God doesn't do deals. Or you could say his deals are one-sided—it's either his way or his way. We can't dictate the terms and conditions of our lives to God. That's because he loves us too much to stand by and watch us crash and burn. We can kick and fight and obstinately go our own way, but we will never know the deep joy of a fulfilling life until we surrender to his will.[1]

In addition to my refusal to be a missionary, since early manhood I had also taken a hard position against adoption. I was

---

1. As the apostle Paul says, "If you go against the grain, you get splinters, regardless of which neighborhood you're from, what your parents taught you, what schools you attended. But if you embrace the way God does things, there are wonderful payoffs, again without regard to where you are from or how you were brought up" (Rom. 2:9, *The Message*).

determined that any child I had would be my own flesh and blood. I had seen a couple of children who gave adoption a bad name, and so I staked out my position to God.[2] "Don't even think about it, God. That's the last thing I'll ever do. Adoption? No! Missionary? No!" And then God started capturing my heart— even *before* I was willing.

Back in 1969, Donna and I had three daughters, Laurie (nine), Julie (five), and Michelle (two). We felt like our quiver was full. Even so, a couple of weeks before Christmas that year, Donna said to me out of the blue, "What would you think about us adopting a boy?" She knew my stance on the issue, so my response shook both of us. "Okay," I replied, "let's look into it." Where did that come from?

Right after New Year's, Donna called an adoption agency and made an appointment to fill out an application for a newborn son. The only request we made was that, if possible, he be a redhead like Donna so that he would fit into the family better. The woman at the adoption agency found that interesting, because a couple had come in the day before and said they'd take any child, including a mentally challenged child, but not a redhead!

Our hopes were dampened somewhat by others, who told us that our chances of adopting were slim, seeing as we already had three children. Priority was given to couples with no children, and there was a shortage of babies available for adoption. After another few weeks, the agency did a background check and, somewhat to our surprise, we were approved. We were told the wait would be seven to nine months. Our girls, who were in on all of this, were getting excited at the prospect of having a baby brother. We decided right away to name him Peter.

The year 1970 dragged a little for us. Then on Friday, November 12, Laurie's ninth birthday, we received the call for which we had waited so anxiously. Would we be able to come in and take

---

2. I've seen a few Christians who give their heavenly Father a bad name too. We believers are all adopted into God's family.

a look at a baby boy? The woman from the adoption agency hastened to add that he was already two-and-a-half months old—and that his birth mother had named him Peter! She said the agency would have let us take Peter home straight from the hospital, but they had wanted him to be checked by a geneticist before they released him, so he had been kept in foster homes for ten weeks.[3] The woman from the agency went on to say that Pete's left ear needed minor surgery, he had sunken cheekbones, and his tear ducts were blocked. But if we wanted to come in and meet him on Monday, we were more than welcome.

Our girls were as wound up as if their birthdays and Christmas had been rolled into one. They barely slept all weekend, doggedly insisting that we take them with us when we went to see baby Peter on Monday.

When the nurse carried him into the waiting room that day, I knew there was no chance of backing out of this deal. The girls went over the top in absolute delight at the sight of this tiny little brother of theirs, all swaddled in blue. Donna and I were just as excited. Signing the papers that released him—conditionally—into our family felt like a mere formality. A few months later, after further checks to ensure that young Pete was being treated well, the adoption was complete. Pete was ours forever![4]

Our girls loved on Pete with all their hearts, literally lining up just to hold him. Laurie, who was already responsible with

3. We found out later that the doctors had been concerned about possible Down syndrome, which proved not to be the case. When we took Pete back to the geneticist for a checkup, the doctor looked us straight in the eyes and said, "This child is not mentally challenged in any way. My wife is having a baby, and I hope he's half as bright as this boy!" When we later had Pete's IQ tested, we discovered he was borderline genius, which we had already suspected! Obviously, Pete was not from our family "barn," genetically speaking.

4. We never did learn what Pete's two-and-a-half months in foster homes had been like. We suspect it may not have been ideal. Nor did we know much about his birth parents, and we knew nothing about his sojourn in his mother's womb. Was it pleasant and comfortable? Or did he endure rejection—and worse?

babies, took special care of him. Despite all this love and attention, Pete was not a "huggy" baby, and he resisted almost all
physical touch.

As he grew older, we learned he was unique in other ways as
well. When he was three, I had to rescue him from the roof of
our two-story house after neighbors spotted him clambering up
the TV antenna. He frequently wandered off and got lost. By the
time he was five, his left outer ear had been corrected, but a hearing loss was discovered, for which he was fitted with a hearing
aid. Pete promptly took off to a friend's house and traded it for a
jackknife! Later, in Hawaii, he forgot to take his hearing aid out
when swimming in the ocean. Turns out salt water and hearing
aids don't mix.

Once when Pete was seven or eight, he decided that his stuffed
animals needed hearts. He lined them all up in a row—thirty or
more of them—and, after duly applying anesthetic, proceeded to
prep them for open-heart surgery by carefully slitting their chests
open. Next, he dipped cotton balls in red food coloring, laid them
out to dry, and then completed the operations by inserting the
implants and closing the incisions with needle and thread. Well,
some of them got closed up, anyway. A fair number lived the rest
of their lives with their hearts in plain view.

Pete was a thinker. Once when he was about eight or nine,
he and his grandfather were commiserating with each other, both
feeling that they didn't fit in. Donna's dad remarked (in jest) to
Pete, "If your grandmother knew what I was really like, she never
would have married me." To which Pete replied, "If my mom
knew what I was going to be like, she never would have adopted
me." This troubled Donna's dad enough for him to tell her about
the conversation. Donna went to Pete right away and read him
Psalm 139, which describes how God knows us intimately, having woven us into our mother's womb. She also told him what
little we knew about his birth parents and the circumstances of
his adoption (though we had been open about that since early on).
Pete then looked at Donna and asked, "Do you think it's possible

that I could be another Billy Graham?" We had always told Pete that he could be anything he wanted and that he was our "chosen son." He often reminded his sisters that they weren't!

By the time Pete was ten, he was having relationship problems with schoolmates. Adults loved him, though, because he was able to carry on an intelligent conversation on a wide range of subjects. Loren Cunningham's secretary, Cathy Assink, adored Pete so much that when she left Hawaii to go home to the mainland, she gave him her car, a tidy little Honda Civic. Pete was just thirteen!

Girls liked Pete too. Since his first crush on a girl, I noticed that any girl Pete was attracted to, and who liked him, was always the sweetest and most popular of girls. Even later, after he left home, the girls—though they may have had little or no Christian influence in their lives—have had sweet spirits despite outward attitudes that fairly bristled.

Often feeling rejected by his peers, Pete developed a love for animals. At one point Pete was given a Double Yellow-headed Amazon parrot named Charlie. Pete cared faithfully for his brightly colored, feathered friend, who merely tolerated the rest of us. (Charlie had a special hatred for Julie, and they frequently sparred.) Pete would sit Charlie on the handlebars of his bike and race around the campus. The parrot loved it, squinting his eyes in the wind and hunkering down close to his best friend.

When Charlie became too difficult to keep in our apartment, we hung his cage in a large tree just outside. With the cage door open all the time and food inside, Charlie was free to climb anywhere. Since his flight feathers were clipped, he could only glide a few feet. Charlie became almost everybody's friend. He spent most of his time perched high up in his stunning, fiery-red-flowered Hawaiian tree, calling out to passersby in his rich, guttural voice, "Hulloh!" Strangers wondered who was up the tree.

Charlie had had a difficult upbringing, which included abuse by his original owner, and occasionally his meanness came out. Sometimes he would yell out, "Sandra! Sandra!" That was the name of the kind woman who had rescued him and then given him to Pete. Charlie's repertoire also included "Lah-di-lah-di-dah," to the tune of "Strangers in the Night," and he would frequently proclaim to one and all, "I'm a bird, I can't talk!" Each day the children from our preschool stopped by during their morning walk to visit and have a chat with Charlie. He was a campus favorite. But it all came to a sad end one day when hungry Charlie, without seeds in his cage, was walking to our apartment to find something to eat and a car accidentally backed over him. Young Pete, all by himself, bravely buried Charlie in a secret place, and we all mourned the loss.[5]

As our challenges with Pete began to grow, I was lying in bed one night agonizing over our decision to adopt for probably the thousandth time and wondering if we had made a mistake. Had we acted out of emotion? Was there a pride factor in me wanting to have a son? Some people had thought we were unwise to do it. What had possessed me to agree to something I had been so set against? Did we blow it, Lord? But what could we do about it now, anyway? Such thoughts and questions stormed around in my head when suddenly I was taken back to the day when I had unexpectedly become open to look into adopting a son. I started to do some calendar-counting from that moment. Pete's birthday was September 3, 1970, though we didn't receive him until mid-November. Working back from September 3 would have put his conception at about mid-December 1969, the very time of my heart change! Bingo! This meant that right at the time when Pete was being woven into his mother's womb, God had done something in my heart to cause such a radical makeover. God saw the spark of a new life beginning and *immediately* chose a family for this tiny pinpoint of potential, of whom even his birth-

---

5. Charlie is actually famous. In 1981 his photo was featured on the cover of the Scripture in Song album *Call To War*. This recording was made just yards from Charlie's tree. And that beautifully blossomed tree, three decades later, often serves as a shady spot for early morning staff prayer meetings.

mother-to-be wasn't aware! The only barrier was my heart, which had needed to change.

This led me to wonder how many families the Lord has asked to adopt babies but who have backed away or refused. Perhaps more significantly, it confirmed to me Psalm 139:13–16, the scripture that Donna had read to Pete.

Oh yes, you shaped me first inside, then out; you formed me in my mother's womb. I thank you, High God—you're breathtaking! Body and soul, I am marvelously made! I worship in adoration—what a creation! You know me inside and out, you know every bone in my body; You know exactly how I was made, bit by bit, how I was sculpted from nothing into something. Like an open book, you watched me grow from conception to birth; all the stages of my life were spread out before you, the days of my life all prepared before I'd even lived one day. (*The Message*)

God knew Pete—and me and you—from the moment of fertilization, no matter the circumstances, ideal or not. I concluded that Pete was our son, a gift from God to our family, and nothing could ever change that.

Once, as Pete and his mom were walking along hand in hand, he said to Donna, "How could a loving God allow me to be put in the womb of a woman who would give me away to a family that had plenty, who then turned around and gave everything they had away? And why is the pathway to hell wide but to heaven narrow?"

Donna remembers: *One day I was walking down the road crying, "Father, where did I go wrong as a mother?" He gently replied, "Where did I go wrong? I'm the most loving Father, and look at my kids." Many times I would wake up in the night fearful and crying for Pete. God would say to me, "I know exactly where he is, and I*

*love him more than you do. Now go back to sleep." What an awesome
Father God we have!*

When Pete was sixteen, he wanted to leave home. High
school hadn't worked out for him. The teachers didn't know how
to deal with a boy who could read books during class, pay abso-
lutely no attention to the lesson, and yet somehow, through a
combination of osmosis and native intelligence, pass all of his
exams—barely. We didn't know what to do. By then Pete was
getting into all sorts of scrapes. Even though he owned a car and
was old enough to drive, I did not feel good giving him permission to get a license. But that didn't stop him from taking the car
anyway! Living in two rooms as we did created constant tension
in the family. For my part, I know I often blew it in the way I
handled the frequent confrontations.

Pete had liked Japan when we visited that nation a year earlier, so it was decided that he would go there for a season. A
YWAM leader we knew over there agreed to mentor Pete. While
Pete had a good time skateboarding with his Japanese friends,
even picking up some of the language, the mentoring relationship didn't work out. So Pete returned to Kona, only to inform us
soon afterward that he was leaving home for good.

The night of his departure was a bit surreal. We planned a
farewell dinner, and I was determined there would be no harsh
words or slammed doors. With Pete all packed and assuring us he
would be living with a friend, we sat down to eat. I don't recall
the things we talked about, but it was civil, and we affirmed our
love for each other. Then we each prayed for him. As Pete got up
from the table to leave—declining a ride to his friend's house—
we all hugged him and wished him well. His mother's parting
words to him were, "Don't forget to brush your teeth!" With
that, he was gone, carrying his possessions in a sports bag slung
over his shoulder.

Only months later did we discover he had no friend's home
to go to that night. Instead, he slept on the beach and went

dumpster diving for food in the morning. Many similar days and nights were to follow. Eventually, he drifted over to the other side of the island, and we lost contact with him completely.

Finally desperate, Pete came home and said he had decided to turn his life back to Jesus. He knew that staying in Kona with all of its influences was not a good option, so he asked if he could go to a Discipleship Training School far away. After we prayed and made some inquiries, we agreed that he should go to Australia and attend the same DTS that his sister Michelle had graduated from two years previously. Pete was desperate to get out of Kona, so the Aussie base leader agreed to accept him a month early.

But wherever you go, *there you are.* Sadly, halfway through the school, the leaders felt they had to terminate Pete's time Down Under and sent him home. This was right at the time we were leaving Kona to return to Canada to start the alumni ministry.

As a painful footnote to the experience, just after he returned to Hawaii, we received a letter in the mail from Pete that he had written just one day before he had been kicked out of the DTS. It was a triumphant account of the wonderful week he had just experienced, how he had been released from bondage to various influences in his life, and how for the first time ever he felt free. He wrote about a mini-miracle where he had no money to buy anything, but he really needed some laundry soap. He prayed to God for help. And when he got back to his dorm, the soap was lying on his bed! On a darker note, he also added the following words: "Please pray for me, because I know the enemy wants me back. There are people in town who can get me what I'm craving right now."

Since we were on the verge of moving back to Canada, Pete decided to stay at a YWAM ministry in Honolulu. As in Japan and Australia, it didn't last long. For the next four years, Pete lived in survival mode, working when he had to, making some friends and being accepted into a culture that we knew little about, a culture where living on the edge was the norm. Inevitably, Pete hit bottom, or what he thought was bottom. He called us from Honolulu saying his life sucked. He had broken up with his girlfriend (for the umpteenth time), the heat was on, and he wanted to come and live with us in Canada. We sent him a plane ticket, and he returned to the land of his birth, which he had visited only a few times since he was six years old.

After a time, I found Pete an apartment and paid his first and last month's rent. He landed a job pumping gas and then moved into a quaint old rental house in the middle of a blueberry farm. By this time Pete had acquired a dog whom he named Buster, plus an old pickup truck. Next he decided to head for an idyllic setting in the woods three hours north of Vancouver. He moved in with a commune of hippies and proceeded to build his own little cabin on the steep slope of a mountain using scrap lumber and anything else he could lay his hands on.[6]

One day back in 1999, after a long time with no word from Pete, Laurie picked up the mail and found a package from the police. Inside was Pete's water-soaked wallet. Tire marks were clearly imprinted upon it. All of his cards and ID were inside. But there was no explanation, just the wallet and its contents. Laurie called every number we knew to call. But no one knew Pete's whereabouts. We could only conclude that Pete was possibly dead, his body lying in some snow-covered ditch. We made a frantic phone call to the police. They called back twenty minutes later to tell us our son was fine and back living in Vancouver, but he didn't want any contact with us. We let out a collective sigh of relief. We were sad that he didn't want to see us, but at least he was alive. Once again, Pete had proven that he was the ultimate survivor.

---

6. Recently, on a clear and crisp winter day, Pete and I drove up to his cabin. He hadn't seen it for a few years, and much had changed. Friends had stayed in it and rearranged things. I was totally impressed with Pete's workmanship: he had scrounged for everything using cast-off scraps of lumber, a pot-bellied stove for warmth and cooking, even picture windows that faced the snowy fir-tree-covered mountains. Pete has always wanted to go and live there permanently—and perhaps he will.

Donna, who now teaches young people all over the world about God's love and how to hear his voice, tells about one time in a Maui Discipleship Training School when she noticed a young guy of about eighteen seated at the back of the classroom. He was dressed in baggy pants with dreadlocks and tattoos. It turned out he was a pastor's son who had run away from home. He walked slowly to the front and, with tears in his eyes, looked straight at Donna. "On behalf of all prodigal sons, I want to ask your forgiveness for what we've done to our mothers." He and Donna wept, as did many others in the room. Then this young man found a basin and washed Donna's feet, and Donna washed his. To this day, he continues to follow in the footsteps of Jesus.

God continues to encourage us. A few years ago a man called and asked for Pete. He had met him years before, when Pete was on the streets. This man said he was now writing a "street Bible" and that Pete knew the Bible better than anyone he'd ever met! Once, when Pete was channel surfing in the middle of the night, looking for horror movies, to his horror he saw Donna on TV. He said next day to his mom on the phone, "I flipped a channel and there you were! Now that was real scary!" Donna had filmed a series on "Listening to God," which had previously been shown across the nation and was now rerunning on late-night TV. Pete went on, "Mom, you're a helluva lot better than all those other preachers!"

Today, we are in contact with Pete, and he even came out to The Hat to visit. Our relationship is much better than it used to be, but is still far from ideal. Though we would not have chosen the pain we have had to experience during this saga, it has allowed us to know the character of God in a way we might never have known otherwise.

I tend to think that the story Jesus told about the Prodigal Son (Luke 15:11–32) is a true story about a real family. It has all the ingredients that make for a good read: tragedy, triumph, and redemption. The tale is preceded by a couple of parables—the lost sheep and the lost coin. Most of us have never lost a sheep, but we've all lost money. And we all know a family that has lost a son. "The Waiting Father" would be a better title for this saga of sorrow than "The Prodigal Son."[7] During the years of waiting for Peter, I have prayed. I have blamed myself—and others. I have been tormented, defensive, offensive, protective, and detached—felt angry, sad, loving, self-pitying, and more. But this father is still waiting for the day when he can throw the party to end all parties and welcome his son home. Dancing? You haven't seen anything yet!

7. In case you are worried, paragraph headings in the Bible were not inspired!

— Chapter 18 —

A Third Love Story

As Donna and I were establishing the ministry of YWAM Associates, Laurie continued in constant pain from chronic medical infirmities. She served faithfully with us, despite frequent interruptions for hospital stays, doctor's visits, and many days when she was confined to bed. This went on for years, and I confess I lost hope of Laurie ever living a normal, healthy life.[1] Ever since she was thirteen, Laurie had wanted to be married and to have children. The latter we knew she would be good at; the possibility of the former ever happening appeared to be slim to none, without God.

Finally, in crisis, Laurie had a major operation to remove all but two inches of her permanently obstructed large intestine. This, together with some personal life counseling, brought a growing improvement in Laurie's overall health. She was approaching her mid-forties, vitally effective and much loved in her role as auntie

1. Mark 5:26 came to me frequently: "She had suffered a great deal under the care of many doctors and had spent all she had, yet instead of getting better she grew worse" (NIV).

to eight nephews and nieces. She had become such an integral part of the ministry that I didn't know what we would do without her. Marriage still did not seem to be on the horizon, but as we were about to learn—again—God's ways are often beyond our understanding.

Early each year, Donna and I would make the long trek Down Under to direct camps for YWAM alumni. These trips were a double blessing. Not only did we get to see parts of New Zealand and Australia and meet many of our alumni, we were also able to spend time with Michelle and Mark and their growing family. In 2005, when Laurie was forty-three, she accompanied us to help serve in the Australian camp.

Peter Worrall, a single man of forty-four who had attended the camps for several years, was also there. Donna, in her inimitable way, asked, "Why are you still single, Pete?" Perhaps, she thought, he might strike up a friendship with Laurie. As it turned out, Laurie and Pete communicated very little during the weeklong camp. But after camp, the two began corresponding via e-mail. Eventually, Laurie asked Pete if he had ever asked the Lord about joining YWAM Associates in Canada. He prayed about it and felt the Lord say he would be in Canada with us sometime in 2006. But because of underwhelming encouragement from his employer, friends, and family, he decided not to come.

The following year, Laurie once again accompanied us to Australia to help with the children's camp program. Early during the week, Pete (who was back again too) asked God if he had missed the boat by not going to Canada. He sensed a release from the Lord to go, and he told Donna and me about his guidance. We prayed with Pete and felt the Lord confirm what he had heard.

The camp speaker that week was David Demian, director of Watchmen for the Nations in Canada. On the final evening, David said to Laurie, somewhat cryptically, "The Lord says to keep the door open." Laurie pondered his words. Was he referring to Pete joining us on staff, or was there something else? On the final morning of camp, Laurie and Pete sat down to talk over coffee. Laurie's ears perked up at the first words out of Pete's mouth: "God has reopened the door for me to come to Canada." Pete planned to join us in late April.

Less than a month after Laurie's return from camp, along came February 14, 2006. Cheekily, Laurie sent Pete an e-card—after not receiving anything from him—and asked, "Are you my Valentine?" That got Pete's attention. From that point on, Laurie and Pete sprinted down the road of romance. We didn't see or hear from Laurie on weekends, but the MSN chat line was humming constantly. I knew a bit about what was going on, but I still had no idea this relationship was rolling along so rapidly.

On March 3, barely seven weeks after they had their first serious conversation, Laurie came over to our apartment. She was not herself. She was fidgety and couldn't settle down. Shortly afterward, Julie and her four kids arrived. Laurie, who would normally be surrounded by the kids, seemed standoffish and nervous. After almost an hour, the phone rang, and the reason for her strange behavior became startlingly clear.

I picked up the receiver. "G'day, Peter!" said Pete in his thick, South Australian drawl. Some small talk followed, and I was about to hand the phone to Laurie when Pete, with an uncharacteristic tightness in his voice, said, "No, I want to talk to you!" Then all of a sudden he blurted out, "May I marry your daughter?" I was dumbstruck. Hadn't I been there before?

With all of the hubbub around me, I withdrew into my office and closed the door. Once again, I had been taken by surprise and couldn't summon up any suitable objection. I meekly mumbled something like, "Yes." My mind was dry mush, incapable of forming any sensible thoughts. Later, I pondered all the clever *bon mots* and cool questions that might have been my rejoinders. How do you plan to support my daughter in the manner to which she has become accustomed? What are your intentions, young man? You can have her—we've kept her too long already!

Only afterward did I realize that Laurie had come across the hall to our apartment following a particularly significant chat session with Pete. Knowing that her sister, nephews, and nieces would arrive soon, Laurie had strongly suggested that Pete "pop the question" to me straight away. Little did she realize Pete needed his customary hot protein breakfast first. Thus, the call came forty-five minutes after Laurie expected it, right in the midst of normal family din.

It wasn't long before we welcomed Pete to Canada to join our ministry team. But more importantly (in God's eyes and ours), the next seven months would serve as an opportunity for Pete and Laurie's relationship to deepen—and be tested. It would also help Pete decide if he wanted to join the Jordan clan. This probationary period passed quickly, and all of us embraced Pete. Their short engagement walk together was characterized by a high degree of maturity and good sense.

December 9, 2006, was the big day—a Christmas wedding at a snow-covered ranch nestled in the beautiful Cypress Hills near The Hat. The event turned into a huge family party with all of our guests seated for the ceremony at round tables already decorated for the dinner reception to follow. After giving Laurie away, I took my place alongside David Demian and helped him officiate the wedding. As the ceremony drew to an end, JoEllyn Wright sat down at the keyboard and surprised us with "Laurie's Song," which she had composed for the occasion. A delicious Chinese buffet dinner was accompanied by an eight-inch-wide, seventeen-foot-long "aisle" cake designed by Graham Kerr.[2]

As I went to bed that night, I reflected that finally the days of blindside phone calls by Australians and South Sea Islanders were over. All my girls were hitched, and I was out of daughters!

---

2. Though Graham and Treena were unable to be with us in person, they had prepared a hilarious three-minute video for all to see. They explained that the bride and groom would cut a slice of the unique cake for each guest; better still, every couple of feet there were $20 bills hidden inside!

Today, Laurie and Pete continue to work alongside Donna and me with YWAM Associates. They now have a baby named Ruth, who was born on November 21, 2008, in Taipei, Taiwan. Her birth mother felt she could not keep her, because Ruth has Down syndrome. For ten years Laurie had tried, even as a single, to adopt a little Chinese girl with this disability. Now her dream has come true. Ruthie has turned our whole family upside down with her beautiful, loving acceptance of each of us. And without exception, everyone immediately accepts her.

Vae and Julie have four children: Leilani, Manu, Tavita, and Hannah. They are still working with YWAM, heading up Island Breeze Canada. They have called and discipled many young people from the Pacific Islands to serve as missionaries among Canada's indigenous peoples.

Michelle and Mark live in Steeltown, Australia (also known as Wollongong), which is famous for its gorgeous beaches. They are raising four children, Daniel, Rebekah, David, and Jonathan. Mark is a mechanical engineer. Michelle ministers in a Christian school, and both of them are involved in the youth program at their church.

Donna and I take little credit for having three daughters in three happy marriages. There is not a shred of doubt in our minds that God handpicked each of their husbands. Ever since the girls were born, we have been engaged in on-the-job-training, and we've learned as we've lived. We have also prayed for each of our kids on a daily basis. We simply did what we could and left the rest up to God.

Sometimes we wonder how the girls would have turned out had we not responded to God's radical call into missions. That, of course, is a hypothetical exercise of little value, but I have often thought that had we not obeyed God by leaving house and family and creature comforts behind, there is no way we would have lived lives of such blessed relational abundance. Regardless of *where* and *when* and *how* and *to what* God calls you, following

Jesus unconditionally is the only way to go. To hear his voice, the voice of the One who wants only the best for his children, and to walk with him step by step through life—ah, that is the path. That is the way.

Faith Is a Frightening Place

Imagine for a moment what was going through the mind of Abraham (known then as Abram) on the eve of his departure for regions unknown. His father, Terah, had already brought the family hundreds of miles from what we know today as Iraq and settled in the city of Haran, in the modern-day Lebanon/Syria region. Then God spoke to Abram saying, "Leave your country, your family, and your father's home for a land that I will show you" (Gen. 12:1, *The Message*). It was time for a farewell party, and all of Abram's family and friends gathered around to wish him well.

"Where ya headed, Abe?" we can imagine his pal Benomi asking.

"Not sure yet," Abram replies, trying to sound positive and self-assured.

"Well, are you going north or south or east or west?" comes the reasonable rejoinder.

Abram straightens up and says with a trace of confidence, "I'll know in the morning—when it's time to leave."

191

And so began the obeying and trusting journey of the man of whom God said, "His faith was credited to him as righteousness." In the morning, he headed south toward Canaan, turning his back on all he had known; God must have told him which way to go. I have to think that at times, even for Abram, faith was a frightening place. Especially when you fast forward several years, where we find Abraham—in direct obedience to God— about to plunge a knife into his precious son, Isaac. At the last second, an angel calls from heaven, "Don't do it!" Abraham's faith was so unshakable that he was certain God would provide a substitute offering. And, of course, God did. But those few moments between pulling out the knife and hearing the angel must have been horrifying indeed.

Jesus' disciple Peter is also remembered for his great faith, even though it was often impulsive and needed time to mature. During a violent storm on the Sea of Galilee, Jesus (who had missed the boat because he was talking to his Father) suddenly appeared to his twelve disciples walking on the troubled waters. Thinking he was a ghost, the men were terrified. But then Jesus spoke to them through the howling gale, "Buck up, men. It's me. Don't be so scared!"

Brave but frequent foot-in-mouth Peter, blurted out, "Well, if it's you, tell me to come to you on the water." Jesus called his bluff with a single word: "Come."

Probably seeking to avoid embarrassment if he didn't act on his quick words, Peter stepped out of the boat, set his foot on the water, and amazingly, he didn't sink!

"Wow!" he must have exclaimed. "Look at me! Look what I can do!" And then, just like a cartoon character who suddenly realizes the true nature of his circumstances, he began to sink. Jesus was quick to rescue him, but once again, we see someone learning that faith is a frightening place to be, especially if you let your eyes slip away from Jesus.

As these and so many other great men and women have learned, faith is lived in the moment. It's about knowing God and his character and resting in that relationship, despite natural disappointments and delays. It's about the seemingly impossible things God calls us to do and his miraculous—and often last-minute—provision to breathe them into existence. It also requires a dogged determination to follow God no matter the circumstances. This means physical action as well as mental and spiritual assent. Faith can be a frightening place, but by knowing God and his character and trusting and obeying him, great men and women throughout history have overcome their fears and pleased God.[1] My family has learned this same lesson numerous times during our sojourn on this earth.

The Bible says men and women don't live by bread alone; we live by every word that comes from God's mouth.[2] If that is true, God will most certainly speak to us through his written Word. He will also speak to us individually by other means about the course of our lives—the direction and guidance that we all need.[3] And yes, that direction will sometimes lead us to a frighteningly impossible place. But like Peter on the water, look who's extending his hand!

Through storms and failures, if I and my family have learned anything, it is this: Listen for God. Trust him. Obey him. That's an unbeatable formula for life.

I sometimes jokingly say that many are called but few are packing. In reality, all followers of Jesus are called. Some may be called into overseas missions, but I believe most are called into something closer to home. Some may also suffer from "Selective Hearing Syndrome" when it comes to a personal word from God. These people only act on the words from God that fit their plans.

"Packing" may be taken literally or metaphorically. To pack and to be ready is really a state of mind. It means being in a constant state of readiness to obey God in detail *as soon as* he speaks.

1. See Hebrews 11.
2. Deuteronomy 8:3.
3. Donna teaches on this subject and has written a manual called *Listening to God*. For information go to http://ywamassociates.com/resources/.

For that to happen, we must *expect* that God will speak, and listen with a heart that is prepared to obey even before we hear the Master's voice. That requires surrendering to a Lord who wants the very best for every one of his kids and who will carry each one through the challenges as well as the great things of life.

So what's next for me and Donna? Retirement? Sorry, but that's not a biblical principle. Though at age fifty the Levites ceased from heavy lifting (dragging sacrificial animal carcasses up onto the altar), they were not sent out to pasture. They graduated to being elders and were valued and honored for their wisdom. How differently we treat elders today in our so-called advanced cultures. Many, perhaps most, are shuffled off like cards into the discard pile of "care" homes.

As long as the Lord gives us strength and (reasonably!) sound minds, Donna and I see no prospect for what is known as retirement. We are blessed with children who, in spite of the price they would have to pay in making space for us, plus all the other considerations, will take us in if the need arises. But we're not quite ready for that yet! And apparently God shares that opinion.

After Donna and I hadn't led missionary training schools for seventeen years because of our other ministry commitments, Loren and Darlene challenged us over breakfast one morning in 2006 to come back to Kona and lead another school. My quick and rather rude retort was, "No way!" Donna chimed in, "We're too old!" As soon as the words escaped our mouths, we realized we had spoken before consulting God. After repenting of our haste, we went away and asked the Lord if he confirmed this invitation. Together, we sensed the Lord saying, "Yes. And furthermore, the school is to be called the 'All Nations–All Generations Discipleship Training School.'" Because of previous ministry obligations, we had more than a year to prepare for the school.

Our first priority was to invite staff to join our *ohana* (family). Blessed with friendships all over the world, we soon had a team from several nations and three generations committed to the school, which was due to commence at the beginning of January 2008. As in a local church (or for that matter, in any business), leaders and staff are the key to a smooth-running and productive endeavor. To the extent that each member loves God, is teachable and flexible, has motivation, humility, purpose, vision, and per-haps most importantly, unity with others, there will be harmony and success throughout the whole structure. If Donna and I can take any credit at all for success, it is because we first asked God in detail who was to join our ohana for each school. Then we basi-cally sat back and let them go for it, ready to encourage and offer counsel—and occasionally correction—as needed.

Through this experience and others, God has shown us that mothers and fathers are desperately needed in missions and in the whole body of Christ. Paul wrote, "There are a lot of people around who can't wait to tell you what you've done wrong, but there aren't many fathers willing to take the time and effort to help you grow up" (1 Cor. 4:15, *The Message*). Why aren't there many fathers (and mothers) who are willing to take the time and effort to help the generations behind them? One problem might be that the following generations, in their headlong rush to make it on their own, don't realize that they should "walk backwards into the future, eyes fixed on the past" (Maori proverb).

It seems as though—in western cultures at least—we actu-ally train people to be old. No matter what life calling (or call-ings) someone may have had, everything points to some pivotal age when it's time to stop, to retire. What this says, in effect, is that you're no longer much use, so take a break—for the rest of your life! The Golden Years have become the "Olden Years," and might just as well be called the "Rusty Old Iron Years," when so many are consigned to the scrapyard of life.

All of that skilled experience, all of that *life* experience, goes to waste and is not passed on to the next generations. The good news is that there are organizations that tap into that experience and gladly receive help and wisdom from, and actively recruit, older people. They offer volunteers all sorts of opportunities to pass on their skills, their knowledge, and their wisdom. In YWAM we have a ministry called Mission Builders that provides opportunities for skilled and unskilled workers in all manners of construction, office work, cooking—almost anything that a willing worker wants to do. By serving in these areas, they free up someone else to carry the Good News to remote parts of the world.

Mankind has always been searching for three things: the fountain of youth, the secret to eternal life, and the ability to fly like a bird. I like to say, "To stay young, hang out with young people. To die young, try to keep up with them!" Want a long life? Even though genetics, the environment, diet, and medical advances can prolong our lives a little, God numbers our days. In the end, it's the quality of life, not the longevity, that counts. As William Wallace says in the movie *Braveheart*, "Every man dies; not every man really lives." The Westminster Catechism states that man's chief end is to glorify God and to enjoy him forever. "Forever" includes all our time on this earth. It is said that Corrie ten Boom somehow ministered to the people who visited her deathbed even though she was in a coma. That's what I call a life lived fully to the end. The Golden Years should be filled with golden wisdom from lives well lived.

When I meet new people, I love to ask, "What is your ministry?" Too often the answer comes back hesitantly, "I, er, teach Sunday School," or "Well, I'm on the worship team." Almost always the answer relates to something that is done in the local church. What I mean when I ask this question is simply, "What do you do?" Whatever a follower of Jesus does *is* his or her ministry. It's the difference between a mere career and a vocation. A career is just something you do to earn a living. A vocation is a job or activity to which you are called by God and through which you channel his grace to the world. Ministry can mean teaching high school, being a stay-at-home mom, flying an airliner, even landing on the moon! Of course, many also serve in some capacity in their local church or a Christian organization. In fact, we're all called to ministry within the local church, whether it be through a musical gift, a serving gift, a friendship gift, a hospitality gift, a tidying-up gift, and many others. But we're also called to ministry within the community in which we live and work. And that ministry should continue throughout our lives on this earth, because no matter how old we get, the fruit of our lives is something that can feed and nourish the next generation.

So what's next? More of the same for Donna as she continues living and teaching her life message, that every Christian can hear God's voice, believe what he says, and then obey him in detail. For me? More writing. I have several themes up my sleeve (or in my heart) that I would love to explore, as frightening as that prospect might be! I will also be expanding and continuing our ministry to the alumni of our mission. And for both Donna and me, our plan is to enjoy and "be there" for our children and grandchildren.

And finally, China—the land of my birth—has become even more significant to me in recent years, and I hope to go back again. This great nation and its peoples are bursting out onto the world's stage and will very soon become the main players in the drama that is the history of our planet. May that "bursting forth" be a righteous one!

I'd like to think that my mom and dad played a tiny part in what we all hope will be a godly spectacle as it unfolds before our eyes. Inside of me is a bit of China. After all, I was "Made in China," and as such, one day I expect to be standing with the largest people group in the middle of that huge multitude gathered before the throne (Rev. 7:9).

See you there?

About the Author

Peter Jordan, along with his wife, Donna, and their children, moved from Canada to the Pacific and Asia for twelve years, helping to pioneer the Youth With A Mission (YWAM) base in Kona, Hawaii. They served in leadership and directed Discipleship Training Schools in both Kona and Singapore. Peter served as assistant to YWAM's founder, Loren Cunningham, for nine years. In 1988 the Jordans started YWAM Associates International, a ministry of encouragement to the hundreds of thousands of missionaries who have served with YWAM.